DWARF AND MEDIAN BEARDED IRISES

Jewels of the Iris World

KEVIN C. VAUGHN

SCHIFFER PUBLISHING
4880 Lower Valley Road • Atglen, PA 19310

Other Schiffer Books by Kevin C. Vaughn:
Sempervivum: A Gardener's Perspective of the Not-So-Humble Hens-and-Chicks, ISBN 978-0-7643-5512-7

Beardless Irises: A Plant for Every Garden Situation, ISBN 978-0-7643-4906-5

Library of Congress Control Number: 2021942414

Designed by Beth Oberholzer
Cover design by Brenda McCallum

Type set in Desire/Helvetica/Minion Pro

ISBN: 978-0-7643-6389-4
Printed in India

Published by Schiffer Publishing, Ltd.
4880 Lower Valley Road
Atglen, PA 19310
Phone: (610) 593-1777; Fax: (610) 593-2002
Email: Info@schifferbooks.com
Web: www.schifferbooks.com

Polly Bishop, Lynn Markham, Bee Warburton, and Jean Witt,
who supported this young hybridizer and steered him
into a wonderful life of plant breeding, and my
parents, who let their son dig up much of the yard for gardens.

It's been a wonderful life.

contents

Preface and Acknowledgments

When I was growing up in Massachusetts, there were some magnificent gardens to visit. Mrs. Corey's, Mrs. Fraim's, and Stedman Buttrick's gardens were estates. They had acres of land and could plant large expanses of garden. Big perennials such as tall bearded irises, Oriental poppies, large-flowered daylilies, and peonies filled these gardens. I still have fond memories of them, but of course such gardens are well beyond the scope of most of us. All these gardeners had help and lots of land to set these plants off, with the beds surrounded by mature trees and shrubs. Mrs. Corey even had a huge glacial boulder as an accent! Most of today's gardens are on a totally different scale. The modern suburban lot does not lend itself to this sort of planting. However, this is not to say that a smaller garden, with plants in scale, can't also be just as striking. This is where the dwarf and median irises can play such an important role. They have the familiar faces of the tall bearded irises, but on a plant and flower reduced in all proportions. These irises fit much more into the way most Americans now garden.

My fascination with dwarf and median bearded irises started in 1964, when the MDB cultivars 'Bee Wings', 'Angel Eyes', and 'Claire' bloomed in the garden at my folks' place in Massachusetts. They were unlike any iris I had seen before, and I thought the bold spots on the falls of 'Bee Wings' and 'Angel Eyes' were amazing. These irises were a gift from our neighbor, Polly Bishop, and she had all sorts of dwarf and median irises in her garden for me to explore. She was also making crosses and taught me how. Little did she know how dangerous that was!

My very first cross was one of 'Curtsy' × 'Angel Eyes', which resulted in my first registration, 'Miss Perky'. Unfortunately, it got a whopping case of virus just after I registered it, but that did not curb my enthusiasm for this group of plants. One of the virtues of a small flower is that you can go as wild as you want with colors and patterns. In a big blossom, it would be gaudy and tacky; in a small flower, it looks surprising but also CUTE and cool. Fifty-seven years later I'm still making crosses on these dwarf and median irises.

New England was a hotbed of iris activity, and Polly introduced me to all the players in the median and dwarf world. Chief among these was Bee Warburton, who was already a phenom when I met her. She gardened like no one I had ever seen; her mission was not to create a beautiful garden but to push the frontiers of the iris world. Bee was also a scholar and, sensing my interest in matters scientific, challenged me with the genetics of the plicata pattern in bearded irises and launched me in a career of genetics, including a PhD from Miami (of Ohio) University.

A number of other people were critical in this early period of my growth, including Lynn Markham, a border-bearded-iris breeder of note. I'm still using her advice to this day. My lines of border bearded irises rely heavily on the foundation she has built. Jean Witt and I corresponded when I was but a kid, and she helped me with my launch into the world of miniature tall bearded irises when she introduced two of my irises, 'Real Jazzy' and 'Tammy's Tutu', which still reside in my garden. Today I'm returning the favor by selecting the last of Jean's seedlings for introduction and using her bloodlines to make new and improved miniature tall beardeds. I still hear Polly's voice in my head when going over my seedlings: "Not your best work, Kevin." She knew right away that enthusiasm with a seedling with obvious flaws would lead to disaster down the road. This

little voice in my head has probably saved me more than any piece of advice.

In 2010, I retired and moved to Salem, Oregon, mecca of the iris world. This is also a special mecca for dwarf and median irises. Here Thomas Johnson, Paul Black, Keith Keppel, and Lynda Miller were creating the dwarf and median irises of the future. Across the river in Washington, Terry Aitken was doing the same. What a privilege and inspiration to be in such a great area. Since moving here, I crank out between one and three thousand new dwarf and median iris seedlings each year and have been able to explore many fascinating lines.

In this book, I want to share with the reader the potential for these wonderful plants, introduce you to some of my favorite cultivars in each class, and show you how to grow them well and produce your own irises by hybridizing new sorts. Like my book on beardless irises, this one is not only to give a guide for a newbie, but also to provide information to seasoned iris growers. I'm confident that you'll find these irises wonderful plants for your garden and they will become your new passion.

Most of this book was written under the quarantine of COVID-19. In this atmosphere I was able to sit down and read over sixty-plus years of *Dwarf Iris Society Portfolios* and *The Medianites*, which gave me a fairly complete picture of these classes of irises. This time of seclusion, so difficult for many, was a good time for me to delve into a subject fully. My bloom season here in the spring of 2020 was a special one, too, and I could think about many aspects of these plants.

Many of the photos in this book were taken in my own garden, but I want to thank Keith Keppel, Robin Shadlow, Paul Black, Mike Sutton, Jack Finney, Olga Wells, Stephanie Markham, Judy Schneider, Liz Schreiner Schmidt, Melissa Shriber, and Terry Aitken for supplying photos of their irises. Phil Edinger, Jack Finney, and Judy Schneider read early versions of several chapters and offered great suggestions for clarity and inclusion. Thank you all for making this a better book. I hope you are pleased with the way I used your photos and comments.

1

Introduction

The genus *Iris* is a diverse one, with species ranging from 4 inches to over 5 feet tall. Despite this diversity, all irises share basic anatomy. Parts are in threes. The upper petals are called standards and the lower petals are called falls. In the center of the flower, often hidden by the standards, are the style arms. Despite these basic formulas, irises vary tremendously in form, colors, and patterns. Indeed, the genus *Iris* was named for Iris, the Goddess of the Rainbow, since irises can be found in almost every color, and many have unusual patterns as well.

The two major divisions of rhizomatous irises are the beardless irises (Vaughn 2015) and the bearded. In bearded irises, the falls have an unusual appendage, the beard—an accumulation of unicellular hairs arranged in a tight cluster directly below the style arms and extending farther down the falls. It is likely that the beard has something to do with insect attraction, because beards are often more colorful than other parts of the flower. If an insect follows the path created by the beard, it will be rewarded by nectar and also potentially pollinate the iris. The signal in beardless irises serves this same function, announcing to insects, "This is where the nectar is!"

Almost everyone is familiar with ubiquitous tall bearded (TB), which are garden staples. These

Example of a tangerine beard on the author's miniature dwarf bearded iris. The unicellular hairs form a cluster that resembles a moustache.

Beardless irises, such as the author's Pacific Coast native iris seedling, have a signal next to the styles that tells the insect where to land and effect pollination.

beauties have stalks over 28 inches in height and with large and ruffled flowers. Intensive breeding work for nearly a century has created plants with flowers from every color from white to black and with intriguing patterns and mixes of color seen nowhere else in the floral world. As lovely as the TB irises are, they are not appropriate for every garden situation. Here's where the dwarf and median bearded irises perform an important role. You have little floral jewels that extend the iris season by six to eight weeks and with great personality. Although these irises are relatively recent on the horticultural scene, they have taken it by storm, since they are not only great garden plants but also incredibly beautiful. Their smaller sizes make them perfect for the smaller garden spots that most of us now have. I should say that I'm not anti-TB; I grow many of them and also hybridize them, but I have found I really like the dwarfs and medians and now concentrate on them. In many ways, I've always liked the miniature versions of plants better. To me they are more charming and perfect than their bigger relatives.

Classification

At present we have five horticultural classes of these dwarf and median irises. This system is based on height of the stalk, season of bloom, and size of the flowers and stems.

The littlest and earliest to bloom are the miniature dwarf bearded irises (MDBs). They are irises up to 8 inches (20 cm) in height and have flowers 2–3 inches in diameter. Originally, the MDBs were up to 10 inches tall, but when the system went metric, the MDBs lost 2 inches. However, flowers with stalks taller than 8 inches often outgrew the MDB class and didn't have the dainty proportions of the smaller members of the class. In general, MDBs don't have branched stalks but often produce multiple stalks on a rhizome, giving a carpet of

A miniature dwarf seedling of the author's with nearly black falls

bloom. MDBs are the group supported by the Dwarf Iris Society, and Caparne-Welch Medal is the top award for MDB irises.

The following four classes are, as a group, called "median irises." They occupy the height range between the dwarfs and the TB irises (8–27 inches or 21–70 cm) and are the focus of the Median Iris Society.

The standard dwarf bearded (SDB) are the next taller and later group, ranging from 8 to 16 inches (21–40 cm) in height with flowers about 3 inches in diameter. The SDBs are from crosses of TB irises with the tiny dwarf iris *I. pumila*, an alpine species or advanced generations of this cross. These irises bloom in dense clumps with flowers resting just above the foliage. Unlike the dwarfs, most modern SDBs have three or more buds. Their hybrid nature makes them very vigorous plants, so they are useful both in rock gardens and mixed perennial beds. Even though the first SDBs were introduced in 1951, they are second only to TBs in number of varieties on the market, and many hybridizers are creating ever more new ones. The Cook-Douglas Medal honors the founders of this class of iris.

The following three groups are all from 16 to 27 inches (41–70 cm), but each differs in bloom and stem sizes as well as bloom season.

The intermediate bearded (IB) irises, as their name implies, are intermediate in size of blooms between the SDBs and TBs (4–5 inches in diameter) and have their peak bloom right between the two groups. This allows for a continuous iris bloom season and to have irises that peak with some of the spring bulbs. Most of the modern IBs

TOP A standard dwarf seedling of Paul Black's 'I'm in Love', showing the abundance of flowers typical of this class

ABOVE A clump of the IB 'Man's Best Friend', showing the beautiful clumps of flowers typical of IBs

are from crosses of TBs and SDBs. Because both of these classes are finished products, the IBs are themselves modern looking and have more buds than the SDBs. They tend to be very vigorous plants. Styles vary greatly, from plants that are barely taller than the SDBs to taller ones with more-elaborate flowers. Most IBs have reduced fertility, but a group of hybrids from the species *I. aphylla* are very fertile and have the highly branched stalk from this species and are fully fertile. Because of their elaborate branching, they start blooming with the IBs but often continue into TB season. The Sass Medal, the highest award for IBs, was named for two trailblazing brothers who greatly popularized the class and produced outstanding varieties in the 1940s.

The miniature tall bearded (MTBs) or table irises bloom later than the IBs and have very small flowers (3 inches in diameter) on stems that are wiry and pencil slim. These were first found in the 1930s as small segregates in the diploid TB seedling fields of the Williamsons in Indiana and were treasured because, unlike bigger bearded irises, they worked well in table arrangements. Flower arrangers still enjoy this class of irises for that purpose. However, they are also extremely rugged garden plants, and their tight clumps with many blossoms and stems make little bouquets in the garden scene. Although problems with fertility hampered development early on, the newer hybrids have high fertility, and great progress has been made with this group. Although the majority of the class is still diploid, hybridizers have used *I. aphylla* to produce tetraploid versions that allow colors and patterns not found in the diploids, chiefly pinks and certain bicolors, to add to the pallet of available colors. These tend to bloom earlier than the diploid MTBs. The

A clump of Chad Harris's lovely veined red MTB 'Black Cherry Sorbet', showing the lovely clump habit of this MTB

Williamson-White Medal, the highest award for MTBs, is named after E. B. and Mary Williamson, who selected the original MTBs, and Alice White, who championed their revival.

Like the MTBs, the border bearded (BB) irises were the result of smaller selections, but this time out of the tetraploid TB seedling patches, and as one might expect, they bloom with the TBs. Many attractive seedlings from TB breeding failed to reach 28 inches in height and were saved to edge beds and for locations where TBs would fall over in excess wind or rain. Although initially bigger flowers as well as more-proportionate ones were considered acceptable BBs, now flowers larger than a combined total of 9 inches (height + width) are considered too big to be acceptable BBs. BBs were once considered "runty TBs," but now, with the addition of fertile IBs and *I. aphylla* to the gene pool, they are often vigorous growers and combine attributes of colors and patterns not even found in the TBs. Harold Knowlton was one of the first to recognize the value of BBs in garden situations, and the Knowlton Medal is named in his honor. These five classes of iris make up the dwarf and median bearded irises covered in this book. We think you will find, as I have, that these are some of the most satisfactory garden plants to be had, and offer something for all tastes.

Two Important Species

Almost all the irises described in this book owe their existence to two species: *I. pumila* and *I. aphylla*. The species *I. pumila* is an amazing plant, varying in color from white to near black and often with a concentrated spot of color just beneath the beard. *I. pumila* is a stemless species that ranges from 3 to 6 inches tall (and with suitably tiny flowers) and has an extreme dwarfing effect. When used in crosses to even very large TBs, the progeny may be as small as 4 inches. The combination of the large genetic diversity of *pumila* mixed with a similar diversity of TBs has allowed for some amazing hybrids. This species is responsible for the production of both the MDB and SDB classes directly, and crosses of MDBs and SDBs to TBs give IBs. Thus, this one species is responsible for three of the classes in this volume and is even involved in some of the BB and MTB pedigrees.

In contrast to *I. pumila*, *I. aphylla* is a branched species, with some forms as tall as 18 inches, although most are much smaller. This species

The white BB 'Princess Bride'

A pot containing the tiny *I. pumila* selection 'Little Drummer Boy'

goes completely dormant in winter, making it extremely hardy in colder climates. Indeed, its name means "without leaves," which refers to its loss of leaves in winter. Colors in *aphylla* are more limited than in *pumila*, but white, parchment (or tinged yellow), and various shades of purple are available. One of the clones, 'Thisbe', a parchment one, proved useful in producing colors other than purple in the hybrids. What *aphylla* contributes to the progeny are thinner, more-flexuous stems with wonderful branching and bud count. Moreover, the progeny of *I. aphylla* are very fertile, allowing for advanced generations that are more difficult, with some of the IBs derived from TB × SDB crosses. The thinner, more-flexuous stalks and consistently smaller size has made for more-graceful BBs. Derivatives of *aphylla* are responsible for fertile IBs, tetraploid MTBs, and some of the most well-proportioned BBs.

What hybridizers have accomplished, starting with these two species crossed onto the tall bearded irises, is just phenomenal.

Lynn Markham's selection of *I. aphylla* named 'Slick', showing the beautiful branching typical of this species

Organization of This Book

Each of the various classes of dwarf and median irises is covered in a chapter that includes the characteristics of each class, the crosses that generate these types, specific uses of the class, a history of hybridizing, and some recommended older and newer favorites. In the "Favorites" category, some of the older ones may be difficult to find commercially, and some may already be extinct commercially but are occasionally offered in sales of the Historic Iris Preservation Society. Because cultural practices for these classes of irises are similar, these aspects are covered in a stand-alone chapter, with caveats to this generality covered in the individual class chapters. Likewise, hybridizing, although with each class's own caveats, is considered in a single chapter, with examples of what is needed in each of the classes.

Bearded irises have jargon associated with them, so accordingly I have added a glossary of these terms. Along with this I have listed a number of sources for dwarf and median irises. Please check out the wonderful nurseries that grow these plants.

When I started to write this book, I used a format of following a cultivar name with the name of the hybridizer and date of introduction in parenthesis. After reading the chapters where I started to use this, I found that it really interrupted the reading flow. Bee Warburton made the same sort of decision when writing *The World of Irises*. The iris Wiki is a source for those wanting dates. In each chapter I have gone more or less chronologically by hybridizer.

Groups That Promote These Plants

Here in the US, two specialty groups have promoted these classes of irises: the Dwarf Iris Society and the Median Iris Society. Membership in these societies gives you the most up-to-date information, as well as providing special sales of plants and seeds available only to members.

The Dwarf Iris Society was founded in the early 1950s by Walter Welch, an enthusiast and hybridizer of dwarf irises. In the early days of the society, test gardens were set up throughout the country to collect varieties and allow hybridizers to send their plants for comparisons with those of other hybridizers. These formal test gardens have morphed into more-relaxed display gardens that feature dwarf iris and are open to visitors. The Dwarf Iris Society conducts surveys of members to form "Popularity Polls" of the dwarf iris most favored by members, which serve as a buying guide for others. *The Dwarf Iris Society Portfolio* is a yearbook that covers all aspects of dwarf irises, from gardening and companion plants to hybridizing.

The Median Iris Society was founded in 1957 by irisarians interested in this group of irises, and this group was instrumental in establishing the four classes of median irises that we have today. As for the Dwarf Iris Society, regional test gardens were set up initially that allowed hybridizers to send in promising seedlings for evaluation and competition. Now the Median Iris Society maintains display gardens in all areas of the country. Their publication, *The Medianite*, is published twice a year and includes articles on new varieties, hybridizing, and use of median irises in the garden. Its symposium of favorite varieties serves as a wonderful purchasing guide. Periodically, mini-conventions, generally scheduled for SDB peak, provide the opportunity to see irises and meet like-minded gardeners.

The Historic Iris Preservation Society (HIPS) promotes all irises of historical significance. Through their Guardian Garden Program, gardeners preserve older cultivars that are less available commercially. Their summer sales of historical irises are a wonderful resource for gardeners who want to gather some of the classic irises. Articles on historical irises are published in their publication *Roots*.

The Reblooming Iris Society promotes rebloom in all types of irises and publishes the *Reblooming Iris Reporter* twice a year. It cover results of rebloom from many areas of the country (rebloom is often a matter of how an iris performs in your climate). Many of these are medians and dwarfs, and some of the most successful rebloomers are medians.

The American Iris Society is the umbrella group for all irises and publishes the journal *Irises* four times a year. The Dwarf and Median Societies are sections of the American Iris Society, although one may belong to all or any one. The American Iris Society trains judges and conducts the voting for all iris awards in North America. Two years after a cultivar is introduced to the market, it is eligible for an Honorable Mention (HM). The award system is tiered so that HM winners are eligible for a more exclusive Award of Merit (AM). The AM winners compete for top award in their class, and winners of the top award compete for the Dykes Medal. Only three median irises—'Brown Lasso', 'Star Woman', and 'Dividing Line'—have won this coveted medal. The American Iris Society also offers a Ben Hager Cup for the best median iris at a convention. Several medians have won other convention awards open to all iris types. In addition to these services, the American Iris Society maintains the iris Wiki, which contains photos and registration information of the many tens of thousands of iris cultivars. A list of all the award winners in each class of irises is also on this website.

Australian, New Zealand, British, French, German, Russian, and Italian societies offer similar sorts of awards schemes and publications. Membership in all these groups will enhance your appreciation for irises of all types and keep you in contact with fellow enthusiasts.

REFERENCES

Vaughn, K. C. *Beardless Irises*. Atglen, PA: Schiffer, 2015. 159 pp.

2

Miniature Dwarf Bearded Irises

For many gardeners, the blooms of the hellebores, crocus, or snowdrops herald the start of the gardening season. For the bearded-iris grower, however, it is the first bloom on the miniature dwarf bearded iris (MDBs). Here in Oregon, this bloom begins in March and doesn't cease until the first week of May. MDBs grow up to 8 inches tall, with blooms no more than 3 inches in diameter. Although the bloom stalks have but one or two buds, the MDBs make up for the lack of buds by producing a sea of bloom on these very compact plants, often producing multiple flowers from a single rhizome. Although the original MDBs were limited to a small range of colors, today's MDBs are available in every color from white to black, and often with bold spots on the falls. Though such bold looks might be considered garish on a bigger blossom, they only make you smile in these small flowers. They look almost unreal. When I first saw them as a child, I was fascinated by their colors and patterns. I still am.

Despite their small size range, the MDB hybrids are a varied lot. Many of the MDBs are derived from Alpine species and are thus very hardy and ideally suited to cold climates. Indeed, in some cases they are almost *too* suited to cold climates, performing less well in warm climates. Older hybrids derived from *I. lutescens* are better for warm climates, as are the ones derived from small segregates from SDB breeding. When I gardened with them in Mississippi, these miniaturized SDBs and the older so-called chamaeiris (now *I. lutescens*) types were the only types that gave good bloom. In Massachusetts and Oregon, I can/could grow them all, though. Because of the diversity of pedigrees in the MDBs, bloom starts in March with the tiny *I. pumila* types, continues with hybrids from SDB × *pumila* crosses, and finishes with the MDBs derived as small segregates from the SDBs. With a proper mix of cultivars, six to seven weeks of bloom is possible. There are even a few MDBs that rebloom.

A small clump of 'Bee Wings', a classic MDB created by Alta Brown

Although one might consider MDBs recent developments on the horticultural scene, there are quite a number of older classic cultivars. One of the so-called pass-along plants that every grandmother grew, the red-violet MDB 'Atroviolacea', is a natural hybrid of *I. lutescens* and *I. pumila*. Being a nearly sterile hybrid, it has great vigor and covers itself with bloom every season with minimal care. It is even found planted on gravesites and around abandoned farmhouses throughout the Midwest. It was so popular it won the Caparne Award in 1952, several hundred years after its introduction to the horticultural world.

Iris lutescens

The species *I. lutescens* is itself a wild hybrid from a cross of the twenty-four-chromosome, tall *I. pallida* (or perhaps a relative such as *I. cengialtii*) with a sixteen-chromosome dwarf plant, possibly *I. attica*, which combined to give a hybrid that ranges in height from 6 to 12 inches, depending on the selection. Thus, some of the selections of *I. lutescens* fall into the MDB group, and some into the SDB group. Originally this species was divided into several other species on the basis of height, distribution, and colors, although genetic and taxonomic studies have lumped these into a single species. *I. lutescens* can grow in relatively warm climates and is widespread throughout the Mediterranean, but it is also hardy even in the cold areas of the Midwest. Early hybridizers of dwarf irises used this species almost to the exclusion of others. There was some progress in form and clarity of colors, but a boost was needed for true advancement. Up to this point, the named cultivars of MDBs were a less exciting lot colorwise, mostly in dirty whites, yellows, purples, and blues.

'Whitone' is a pure *I. lutescens* cultivar in white with a flush of pale yellow in the falls.

The *I. pumila* Revolution

Although there was some crossing of MDBs before the 1940s, a real boon to the class occurred when Bob Schreiner imported seed of pure *I. pumila* from Austria, Romania, and the Crimea. He named two of the seedlings 'Sulina' and 'Carpathia' for the areas of Romania near their collection site, and one of the Crimean seedlings 'Nana', a small red violet. Although none of the seedlings from the Austrian *pumila* seeds were named by Schreiner, the plants were sent to Paul Cook, who began using them in crossing. It should be noted that although plants that were marketed as "pumilas" were grown for many years before this, they were in fact not *I. pumila* but mainly *I. lutescens*, which are much-larger flowers.

One reason *I. pumila* was such a genetic powerhouse was because of its origins. Karyotype analysis by Randolph and Mitra (1959) indicated that *I. pumila* was, in fact, a hybrid of two closely related sixteen-chromosome species, *I. attica* and *I. pseudopumila*, but containing full sets of chromosomes from both parents, giving it a chromosome number of thirty-two. This genetic diversity allowed not only for this extreme variety of flower colors, but also the potential for much-greater range than both of its parents, growing as far west as the former Yugoslavia and Austria and as far east as the Crimea. In each of the localities, the types differentiated further with very petite clones from the East and a very unusual but genetically interesting form found on Crete, named 'Cretica', that proved to be a critical cultivar in bringing other

colors and patterns into the dwarfs. Not all *pumilas* had thirty-two chromosomes, and many of the dainty Russian accessions had thirty or thirty-one. Randolph and Mitra (1959) found that in one of the Russian clones, chromosome 2 of the thirty-two-chromosome *pumila* had added a piece of (or most of) another chromosome so that all the genetic information of the thirty-two-chromosome pumilas were present, but with one or more lost chromosomes.

The morphology of *I. pumila* is unique too. In most clones, there is no stem, but rather the perianth is formed directly on the ground and expands so that the flower rises above the foliage. Similarly, the pod forms at ground level. Although there are no branches to the flower, other flowers, up to eight, can be seen rising from a single rhizome, ensuring a longer season of bloom. On the bloom itself, a huge color range from white to black could be had (Warburton 1968), although what is available commercially today is much less. In addition, *I. pumila* contributed a spot to the falls in most cultivars. The spot is a round concentration of color right below the beard. The spot could occur on any background color, giving rise to miniature variegatas, amoenas, and neglectas. Beard colors were mostly whites or blues, but yellow-bearded ones were found in later seedling patches. These yellow-bearded pumilas were critical in producing tangerine-bearded dwarfs in later generations.

Besides this genetic diversity, *I. pumila* has an amazing ability to even miniaturize the progeny from crosses to tall bearded varieties. Because of its tetraploid composition, it produces fertile amphidiploids when crossed to other tetraploids, and even first-generation hybrids of tall bearded × *pumila* occasionally gave very small seedlings, such as the first MDB plicata 'Knick Knack'.

A clump of the tiny MDB 'Hobbit'

The introduction of *I. pumila* to the gene pool of the MDBs was a revolution not only for the MDBs but for all of the medians and dwarfs. In each chapter for each class of iris, you will see how some derivatives of this species have been helpful in producing new hybrids.

Garden Uses and Culture

Uses for the MDBs are many. Because of this small size and their Alpine connections, they are perfect inhabitants of rock gardens, fitting in with the Alpine flora but adding colors and patterns seen nowhere else in that flora. For the purist rock gardener who doesn't prefer hybrids, the many varieties of *I. pumila* offer some wonderful colors and patterns not seen in other rock plants. I have even grown a mix of pumilas from seed, and almost all of them were usable plants for a rock garden, and in a nice variety of colors and patterns.

In my garden in Oregon, I use the MDBs to edge plantings of larger irises and in beds of their own, especially those where larger irises would look inappropriate, such as dooryard beds and small or especially narrow beds. Some of the tougher MDBs can be grown in the mixed border, although they can't take being smothered by their neighbors. Generally, keeping companion plants on the small side and spacing them away from the MDBs gives the best results in a mixed border. They look great next to some of the smaller *Sempervivum* and *Sedum* cultivars. My friend Lynn Smith grows beds of *Sempervivum* in raised beds created by stacking cement blocks to form an edge, and with the edges of the beds containing small cavities created by the holes in the cement blocks. These are planted with MDBs, and the MDBs love it. The perfect drainage, lime wash from the concrete, and a pocket not competing with other species provide an ideal environment. Similar sorts of beds of just cement blocks could hold a lovely collection of MDBs and in a fairly limited space.

MDBs are shallow rooted, and newly planted divisions are vulnerable during winters where

The MDB 'Prodigy' in a rock garden setting

freezing and thawing can heave them from the soil. In Massachusetts, in a cold Zone 4 garden, I found that a rock or brick placed on the rhizome was sufficient to keep the plant from heaving. After the first year, most plants settle in and don't require this extra protection. Alternatively, a bed can be covered with Remay or other frost blanket coverings after the ground has frozen. If it is placed on before the ground is frozen, the soil won't freeze, and the covering may be a way for voles and mice to attack your plants. When I lived in Massachusetts, I put a half-inch layer of pine needles around the MDBs, and that also seemed to insulate the plants from the worst effects of winter heaving. Salt marsh hay is very clean and is great winter mulch for all types of irises. My neighbor in Massachusetts, Polly Bishop, provided the dwarf irises with a living mulch of violas, stemming from a cross she made between pansies and Johnny jump-ups. Over the years these self-sowed among the irises and provided some protection as well as blooms through much of the year. The viola flower colors are in a range that worked well with bearded-iris flowers. Bee Warburton even selected a special strain of Johnny jump-ups with a white rather than yellow center that she thought went perfectly with her irises.

Transplanting MDBs should be done more quickly than other types of bearded irises. Because they have smaller rhizomes, they are more apt to dry out than even the SDBs. Some growers even ship MDB rhizomes with damp toweling around the roots, resulting in less desiccation. If plants are received in the mail dry, I will soak them for several hours in a shallow container of water (just submerging the roots) in a shaded area to let the plants rehydrate before planting. This tiny bit of soaking seems to get them started more quickly. When digging and transplanting in my own yard, I dig, divide, and transplant to a new site, all in one day. Because dwarf irises have a more limited root run, I generally add some fresh soil when they are transplanted and water with a transplant type of fertilizer to give them a fresh start. Generally dwarfs want full sun, but I grow some even here in Oregon with a half day of sun. When I gardened in Mississippi, at the edge of the area where MDBs are successfully grown, the beds that received high shade—not dense shade, but rather shade from deciduous trees that had been limbed up so that air circulation was still good. The irises had higher light all winter and through the time they were blooming but were kept relatively cooler under shade in the summer.

Because MDBs like a cold winter, they aren't the best performers in very warm climates. Some of the iris growers plant them in pots and use them as one-season annuals, since their flower buds are set in the North and they bloom well for one season. Because MDBs are cheap relative to other bearded irises, they can be treated as throw-aways or the rhizomes sent to friends in the North.

Kinds of Crosses That Generate MDBs

Pure pumilas

Seedlings of pure *I. pumila* are the earliest of the bearded irises to bloom and are very charming plants. What they lack are the more sophisticated forms of some of the hybrids that incorporate genes from tall bearded irises into their pedigree. Still, the pure *I. pumila* offers an incredible range of colors, and many have contrasting spots of color next to the beard. The blue color in *pumila* is much bluer than in other bearded irises. Despite their charm, there has been relatively little attention given to pure pumilas of late, and many of the older cultivars that were critical in the breeding both of dwarfs and medians have been lost. Partly that's because these plants perform best in cold climates and are apt not to bloom in warm winter climates, whereas the hybrids grow in a much-wider variation in climates. Ben Hager did develop a strain of pumilas that were adapted to the warm Central Valley of California, so it is possible to overcome this climatic barrier.

SDB and chamaeiris × pumila

When *pumila* is crossed with the forty-chromosome SDBs or chamaeiris varieties of the same genetic composition, the flowers that are created have the form of the larger varieties but the daintiness of the *pumila*. Because of their hybrid nature, they are very vigorous and hardy plants, growing over a wide range of the country. The old natural hybrid 'Atroviolacea' is probably the oldest of these sorts of hybrids. Many of these varieties were produced during the heyday of the dwarf iris movement, including the ever-popular yellow-with-black-spot 'Bee Wings' and delicate blue 'Claire'. The problem with these hybrids was their relative infertility. They were not completely sterile, however, and probably needed to be used more as parents. Both 'Bee Wings' and 'Claire' set pods for me as a kid, so I'm sure there is some fertility in many of this group. The Willotts used this sort of cross in many of their introductions, because they had well-developed breeding programs both in the SDBs and the pure pumilas. Combining these two lines produced a number of award-winning plants. Because of their hybrid nature, they bloom about halfway between the pure pumilas and the SDBs, filling an important gap in the season.

Small Derivatives of SDBs

As the standard dwarfs were being intercrossed, many of the seedlings had smaller flowers and shorter stalks, putting them in the MDB size range. Ben Hager interpreted this as such: "The pumila parent was becoming more dominant in these hybrids." *I. pumila* has four chromosomes that will pair with the TB chromosomes, and it has been thought, although not proven, that these SDB-derived MDBs might have an extra *pumila* chromosome or a portion of one, which might make for a plant smaller than a typical SDB. (The genes for plant size are on these four chromosomes that pair, further giving credence to this theory.) Crosses between these SDB-derived MDBs tend to give mostly MDBs, although taller SDBs also appear in these crosses. Almost all the small pinks and plicata MDBs are from this kind of cross. Although they bloom mostly with the SDBs, they tend to be earlier than the bulk of the SDBs, possibly because their shorter stalks require less expansion before blooming. If you can grow SDBs in your garden, you can grow this group of MDBs.

Tet MTB × pumila

Ben Hager was one of the true revolutionaries in the breeding of all types of irises. He became increasingly frustrated that the best MDBs were the nearly sterile thirty-six-chromosome SDB × *pumila* type of cross. Ben had already used the species *I. aphylla* to create a new class of tetraploid MTB, and he thought about the possibility of creating MDBs by crossing the tetraploid MTBs with *pumila* and getting a forty-chromosome strain that would be fully fertile. Although not all the progeny from such crosses are MDBs, many are, and they tend to be a little more reliably in-class than those derived strictly from SDB crosses. These crosses and their advanced generations gave Ben a whole series of wonderful MDBs in a wide variety of colors and including several Caparne-Welch Medal winners. Moreover, because this group is fertile and gives fertile offspring with the SDB-derived MDBs, they have proven to be useful parents, giving rise to predominantly MDBs.

Miscellaneous Other Approaches

Although the approaches listed previously account for the majority of available MDBs, other workers

'Footlights', an MDB from tetraploid MTB × *pumila* breeding

experimented with other species. Most of these were one-off hybrids, but a considerable early effort combined the bright-yellow *I. humilus* (then often grown as *I. arenaria*) with chamaeiris cultivars. All these cultivars are sterile, or nearly so, but added bright-yellow and even "pink" shades to the MDB palette of colors. 'Promise' was one I grew as a kid, and it was a very nice flower and won the Caparne Award. Donna Simonson did find that one of these, 'Keepsake', would make seed, and even raised a second-generation seedling, but that was clearly the exception to the rule. Hybridizers have been very imaginative in using a number of other iris species in creating MDBs. Many of these are sterile or of limited fertility, although some have been used in further breeding. One of the more popular of these hybrids is the tiny 'Velvet Toy', from a direct cross of *pumila* with *aphylla*. It is a tiny, branched dwarf that reblooms even in New England. 'Buddha's Song' is a hybrid of *I. suaveolens* and has the overlarge standards and tucked falls from its parent as well as the dominant amoena pattern. It is one of the few diploid dwarf irises to be introduced.

History of the Miniature Dwarf Bearded Irises

As in many aspects of the horticultural world, the history of MDB hybridizing started with the British. William John Caparne was an artist of some renown, and the great iris hybridizer Sir Michael Foster had him paint many irises. After painting the Foster plants, Caparne himself became interested in irises. He eventually moved to the Isle of Guernsey and established both an artist studio and a small iris nursery. He specialized in dwarfs and also produced intermediates from crossing his dwarfs with tall bearded irises, making him sort of the godfather of all that is in this book. However, many of his introductions were MDBs, and these were produced at a time when interest in dwarfs was not high. The American Iris Society recognized Caparne's pioneering work by naming one of the first "other iris" medals for him in the early 1950s.

Elsewhere in Europe, the nursery of Goos & Koenemann (G&K) was working at producing dwarfs in Germany. As with Caparne irises, most if not all of these are from chamaeiris forms. Some of their hybrids may have been derived from the Caparne varieties, since G&K imported both named varieties and seedlings from Caparne. Max Goos was the hybridizer in the group, and one of his first hybrids was the appropriately named 'Compacta', a blue-purple that was barely 6 inches tall. As with Caparne, the G&K nursery also used the dwarfs to cross with the TBs to produce intermediates. Having a continuous season of bloom was of paramount importance to Goos as well. Most of the dwarf irises from G&K were lost during the two world wars, although an effort has been made to collect others of their hybrids in botanical gardens in Germany.

The first American dwarf iris specialist was Sam Burchfield, who introduced a number of dwarf irises in a relatively short time during the mid- to late 1920s. His Hudson Valley Nursery price list carried not only his own introductions but also a number of introductions of other hybridizers. Although Burchfield used only chamaeiris types, the irises he introduced had much-improved colors and forms compared to their predecessors, including finally some really good yellows and purples that were grown long after their introduction: 'Endymion' (a red with red flowers and rhizomes), classic light-yellow 'Harbor Lights', and silvery white 'Silver Elf'. A dark-gold seedling of fine form was subsequently named 'Burchfield' in his honor and was his most enduring creation. Unfortunately, Burchfield did not register his irises with the American Iris Society, and nothing is known of their breeding.

The Sass brothers, Hans and Jacob, were very interested in producing hardy irises because they gardened in Nebraska, where winter conditions often killed more-tender cultivars. They were prolific hybridizers and won four Dykes Medals for their TBs. The dwarf irises derived from chamaeiris could take all that the Nebraska climate could dish out, and were used heavily in crosses both to other dwarfs and also to TBs to create hardy intermediates. Among the triumphs of their MDB breeding programs were the red-black 'Tony', deep-yellow self with nice form 'Sound Money', pinkish-lavender 'Pink Mauve', and light red-violet 'Rose Mist'. 'Sound Money' won the very first Caparne Award in 1950. The next generation of the Sass family, Henry, introduced the last and probably greatest of the chamaeiris type MDBs, 'Black Baby'. It won the Caparne Award in 1962 and was a treasured breeder especially for SDBs, one of the few chamaeiris involved in SDB breeding.

'Ablaze' is one of the wonderful hybrids of Walter Welch that combine chamaeiris with *pumila*.

Paul Cook was a true experimentalist in the iris world. Although he bred TBs and won three Dykes Medals for his efforts, he searched many of the dwarf irises, at first to find possible sources of true blue color for the TBs, and later to develop bitone and bicolor irises. In his MDB-for-MDB's-sake work, he was the first to bring *I. humilus* into the gene pool, crossing them to chamaeiris, especially the cultivar 'Socrates'. These resulted in the bright-gold 'Keepsake', the lavender-pink 'Promise', and red 'Tampa'. These remained popular for years, and 'Promise' won the Caparne Award in 1966. Unfortunately, these hybrids are sterile or nearly so. Paul was the first to make TB × *I. pumila* crosses to create the SDB cross, but one of his first seedlings (from 'San Francisco' × *I. pumila*) was used extensively by MDB breeders, especially Walter Welch. Paul obtained seed and plants of *I. pumila* from Robert Schreiner and worked with these plants to produce even-bluer ones. His 'Sky Patch' was considered one of the closest to true blue. His other great contribution to dwarf iris breeders was a seedling he shared, numbered 1546. It was a magical parent and was much used by other MDB breeders. It is the parent of Welch's H503, which was an invaluable breeder, and it imparted better form to most of its progeny.

Walter Welch was a controversial figure. He almost single-handedly started the Dwarf Iris Society (DIS), served as its editor and round-robin director, and produced a number of important hybrids. However, he waged a battle with the American Iris Society (AIS) over awards, judges, and classification and created an alternative to the AIS awards systems and appointed specific dwarf judges. Thankfully, these considerations are no longer issues, and DIS is fully integrated as a section of the AIS. His hybrids involved virtually all approaches to dwarf iris breeding: in the pure (or nearly pure) *I. pumila* breeding lines was 'April Morn', a strong and clear blue self and a very good parent; 'White Mite', the first clear white without yellow overtones and perhaps the most perfect blue *I. pumila* of its day; and 'Atomic Blue'. In the pure chamaeiris lines, his 'Whitone', a white/ivory bitone, had probably the best form of all the MDBs of this type. 'Orange Glint' was the nearest to orange of these types. Red-purple 'Blazon', with a startling contrasted gold beard, was a very popular MDB and won the Caparne Award in 1955. His most-important hybrids combined different species groups, however. Combining the *I. pumila* lines with either chamaeiris or recently created SDBs of Paul Cook's produced MDBs with more sophistication and variety of colors and patterns. Bright variegatas 'Primus' and 'Ablaze' (great name!), light-blue-over-yellow 'Dream Child', greenish-gold 'Dirty Face', and black-violet 'Little Villain' are outstanding examples. The dark amoena 'Sparkling Eyes' combined SDB, chamaeiris, and *I. pumila* into a totally new look; its seedling 'Heart's Content' was an even-darker amoena and a better-growing plant. 'Heart's Content' was one of my favorites as a kid. 'Cherry Spot' was the first red amoena among the dwarfs and garnered Walter the 1960 Caparne Award. Perhaps Walter's most enduring introduction is 'Fashion Lady', a cross of the SDB 'Baria' and his own 'Orange Glint'. 'Fashion Lady' was a revolution in form and had a lovely soft lemon-yellow color and won the Caparne Award. Among his later introductions, 'White Light' is one of the few clear whites among the MDBs and has fine form. When the Caparne Award was raised to medal status, the American Iris Society renamed the award the Caparne-Welch Medal, perhaps completing the circle of bringing the dwarfs back under the AIS umbrella.

Walter Marx was the last hybridizer who used only traditional chamaeiris types in his breeding program. Chiefly these involved the Burchfield cultivars and a choice collection of *I. lutescens* provided by the great Swiss plantsman Henri Correvon. This mix of cultivars and the Correvon plants gave some of the best of this type yet produced, including the blue bitones 'Blue Flash' and 'Blue Mascot', rose-red 'Heatherbloom', and golden-yellow 'Golden Carpet'. His 'Beauty Spot' was one of the first aril-bred dwarf hybrids and won the Caparne Award in 1953. When Leona Mahood visited his garden in the early 1950s, she admired some of his work but was horrified when he told her that he was trying to select for larger flowers. This seems not to have happened, so maybe Leona's admonishment squelched that effort.

Alta Brown was a powerhouse of all the median and dwarf iris classes. Along with her husband, Rex, she ran a nursery, Brown's Iris Garden, which not only introduced Alta's hybrids but also disseminated hybrids from others. Alta was one of the first to make crosses between improved *I. pumila* selections with the newly created SDBs, and her steady stream of introductions of pure pumilas, small SDBs, and hybrids between them were often dubbed with a "stable name" of "April," which is also when these irises bloomed for Alta. Yellow bitone 'April Accent', yellow amoena 'April Charm', white 'April Frost', and bright variegata 'April Var' all are fine examples. (Not all irises' names starting with April are Alta's, because it is not a trademark.) Some of Alta's finest MDBs are from crosses of the new SDB class and *pumila* selections of hers and others. Among the most enduring is her 'Bee Wings', which has tawny-yellow flowers with a distinct brown-toned black spot on the falls. It is a prodigious increaser and heavy bloomer. These characteristics made 'Bee Wings' a shoe-in for the 1963 Caparne Award. Nearly true-blue 'Claire' combined the very blue SDB 'Fairy Flax' and one of her blue *pumila* seedlings. A further cross of 'Claire', with Alta's blue *pumila* 'Cute Capers', resulted in the nearly turquoise 'Claire's Joy'. Often the SDB × *pumila* crosses were nearly sterile, so obtaining a seedling backcrossed to *pumila* was an exciting development. Alta had an extremely well-developed SDB program, and small segregates were saved for breeding the MDBs. It was these sorts of crosses that allowed her to bring plicatas and tangerine pinks into the MDB lines. 'Mini Plic' was one of the first MDB plicatas and had better form than many of this era. Crossed with a sib, it produced the even more striking 'Kid Sister' and 'Mini-Spark'. 'Baby Pink' was the first of the MDB pinks on the market, and many other workers used it to produce a strain of MDB pinks. By its pedigree it should be a thirty-six-chromosome hybrid because it contains a backcross to the *pumila* 'Carpathia', but it maintained at least some fertility. Alta's 'Irish Doll' is a great, truly green amoena from crossing the SDB 'Green Spot' with a white chamaeiris seedling. With this pedigree, 'Irish Doll' was grown easily in most parts of the country and won the Caparne Award in 1969. Within the full *pumila* hybrids, 'Albino Doll' represented one of the first glaciata hybrids in any median or dwarf classes and is a pure white from selfing 'Cretica', the tiny purple *pumila* from Crete. Alta and Rex sold their nursery to Jack Boushay, who continued to introduce the last of Alta's hybrids and to carry on her lines.

Bennett Jones was one of the early hybridizers both of miniature dwarfs and median irises, and his first introductions, as well as some of his last, were MDBs. His early efforts were to combine the Cook SDBs, chamaeiris cultivars, and *I. pumila*. One of his first successes in these lines is the beautiful 'Angel Eyes', a white with a turquoise-blue spot. It won Bennett his first Caparne Award in 1961. 'Angel Eyes' was one of the irises that first enchanted me with this group of plants, and unlike many of these mixed-pedigree irises was easily fertile as well. 'Polka Dot' is similar in pattern to 'Angel Eyes', but with a navy-blue spot rather than a turquoise one. 'Chicken Little' is a sibling to 'Angel Eyes', but in a lovely creamy yellow with nice form. 'Ducky Lucky' is white with a duck-gold spot. I guess Bennett thought that "Turkey Lurkey" may have gone too far as a name to complete the "Chicken Little triumvirate"! For many years Bennett turned his attention to SDBs and BBs, but later in his career his inbred orange and green amoena SDB lines began segregating out a number of well-formed MDBs as well. 'Pretty Pixie', a green-toned amoena with bright beard, and pastel-orange amoena 'Tooth Fairy' came out of these lines and are useful parents for infusing form into MDB lines. 'Tooth Fairy' won a Caparne-Welch Medal for Bennett.

Leona Mahood was one of the major players in the Dwarf Iris Society; she maintained the Northwest Test Garden for dwarf irises for many years. In her garden you could see representatives of the cutting edge of dwarf iris. She was also a hybridizer of some renown. Her hybrids were derived mostly from crosses of SDBs and *pumila*, although she did pure pumilas and small SDB-derived work as well. Her first major break was the pastel neglecta 'Grandma's Hat'. Her series of orchids were especially welcome because they provided pinkish tones before MDB tangerine pinks were available. 'Dream Stuff' and 'Orchid Flair' were my favorite, a clear shade of orchid, probably due to the *pumila* parent 'Cretica'. 'Shamrock Fan' is a tiny green amoena out of SDB breeding. One of her last hybrids, 'Red at Last', was a very good red for its day, and it still graces my garden. For years, she introduced hers and other breeders' MDB through the Northwest Hybridizer's group catalog when sources of dwarfs were few.

Bee Warburton's work with the small irises started from her interest in using irises in the rock garden, but she quickly turned to hybridizing. Although Bee Warburton's primary breeding interests were in the SDBs and IBs, she also contributed to the development of MDBs. Her first MDB introduction, 'Blue Doll', is still with us, since it's an incredibly vigorous iris, one of the early hybrids from SDB × *pumila* crosses. 'Sky Caper' is the same sort of cross but a really blue flower, something Bee was chasing in her SDB lines as well. 'Already' is a great small maroon red with deeper fall spot from SDB × *pumila* breeding. Besides these three hybrids, Bee also introduced the pure *pumila* 'Lemon Doll' and the red-violet 'Tiny Taurus', which is the only introduced hybrid involving *I. taurica*.

David Sindt was the son of Gus Sindt, the owner of median and dwarf specialist nursery Riverdale Iris Garden. Because of this exposure to the best of dwarf irises available, David produced a series of MDBs from virtually every approach to MDB hybridizing, It is truly unfortunate that he passed away so young; he had

already created some wonderful cultivars, three of which won the Caparne Award. In the pure *pumila* lines, bright-gold 'Sun Sparkle', light-yellow 'Gay Sunshine', and very red 'Garnet Gleam' are outstanding colors and shapes for pure pumilas. Two of his introductions descend from the marvelous Welch hybrid 'Sparkling Eyes': the cocoa-brown amoena 'Crème de Cacao' and the vibrant neglecta 'Wild Blueberry'. Both of these were much-better growers than their parent. Many of his most popular varieties combined his *pumila* lines with the best SDBs. These include 'Zipper', a tawny gold with bright-blue beard, and a child of the famous blue-bearded brown SDB 'Gingerbread Man'; bright-gold 'Nuggets'; and soft lavender 'Far and Wee'. In the small SDB approach are the clear white glaciata 'Snow Cub', stitched plicata 'Quip', and one of my favorites of David's, the perfectly named 'Robin's Nest' with robin's-egg-blue flowers.

For many years, the work of Dorothy and Tony Willott defined the MDB class. They worked both with SDBs and MDBs, so they had lots of SDBs to cross with *pumila* to create classic MDBs. For these efforts they won three Caparne-Welch Medals and the American Iris Society's Hybridizers Medal. A memorial garden planted with their hybrids in Cleveland commemorates their contribution to the iris world. Among the classic MDBs, their Caparne-Welch Medal winner 'Alpine Lake' remains one of the most endearing. It is a clean blue amoena with very nice form, and one that grows well across the country. After many years of propagation, this cultivar does occasionally show virus streaking in the falls. The *pumila* parent of 'Alpine Lake' is a Greenlee seedling that the Willotts used in many of the crosses. 'Pussytoes' is a lovely shade of green. Although many so-called green irises are a messy mix of tawny brown over yellow, 'Pussytoes' is a much-cleaner color,

'Blue Doll' is one of Bee Warburton's many wonderful hybrids and is a vigorous and enduring plant.

and the green is not confined to the spot area. The 2005 Caparne-Welch Medal winner 'Little Drummer Boy' is a pure *pumila* and may be the cleanest blue amoena *pumila* ever created. Its pedigree includes a number of the great *pumila* cultivars. Of the other Willott MDBs, five of my favorites are the richly colored and strongly spotted 'Beachwood Buzz', the very vigorous cream 'Saucy Sprite', the tiny plicatas 'Pixie Kisses' and 'Pixie's Sister', and the strong and vigorous blue-purple 'Pixie Pirate'.

Lynda Miller lived in the heart of the dwarf iris movement near the giants in this field, Walter Welch and Earl Roberts, so it was only natural that she would take up growing and hybridizing the MDBs. Lynda has introduced pure pumilas, reduced-size SDBs, and hybrids involving multiple approaches. Among her pure *I. pumila* types are the vigorous blue amoena 'Daring Eyes', variegata 'Bee Early', and neglecta 'Hobbit'—all are outstanding plants, with better form and clearer colors than traditional pumilas. In the tangerine lines from small SDBs,

TOP 'Small Token' is one of the Lynda Miller's many fine MDBs.

BOTTOM Terry Aitken's brilliant 'Hot Coals'

TOP 'Hobbit' is a well-formed blue *pumila*.

BOTTOM The bright 'Hot Tip'

the cotton-candy-pink 'Candy Fluff' and the siblings 'Oh Grow Up' and 'Minifigs' are all well in-class and have improved form. The latter two arise from Keith Keppel's outstanding orange MDB 'Fission Chips'. Lynda has won the Caparne-Welch Medal three times for the variegata 'Squiggles', the bird's-egg-blue 'Scruples', and the neglecta 'Snuggles'. Lynda likes small names for her MDBs, and these iris names seem somehow perfect for the MDBs for which they are named. She has brought her MDB program to Oregon and is continuing to turn out wonderful in-class MDBs here. One of my favorite of her new ones is the quite red 'Small Token'. Good red dwarfs are as rare as hen's teeth, so it is especially pleasing to have a good red color and fine habit. 'Pixie Fuzz' is a tiny raspberry orchid with a bright-orange beard. The foliage and clump habit is very petite, but the colors are so bright that it makes a great statement.

Terry and Barbara Aitken own Aitken's Salmon Creek Iris Nursery in Vancouver, Washington. Terry is the hybridizer, and Barbara runs the nuts and bolts of the nursery. Terry's first successful MDB introductions were fallouts from his SDB breeding programs: 'Grapelet', grape with darker spot, 'Chubby Cherub', pastel cream lemon with blue beard. Both of these had the form of the SDBs on a more diminutive plant, and both won the Caparne-Welch Medal. Terry incorporated the Hager MDB 'Self Evident', derived from tet MTB × *pumila* lines in both his SDB and MDB crosses. From these crosses an outstanding series of amoenas and bicolors was obtained: amoenas 'Aquadoodle', 'Tiny Beacon', and 'Boink', and warm bicolors 'Hot Coals', 'Hot Tip', 'Fairy Firefly', and 'Gecko'. These all are good growers and very good parents for MDBs. Terry introduced Bennett Jones cultivars and used them heavily in breeding. As with Bennett, this line produced many smaller irises, and his bright 'Hot Buttons' and award-winning 'Tiny Titan' are two outstanding examples from Bennett's orange lines. The most recent of these, 'Orange Squeeze', is amazingly bright.

For years, Paul Black was the co-owner of MidAmerica Iris Garden, and his devotion to the dwarf and median classes earned him many awards, including several Caparne-Welch Medals. All of Paul's introductions are from reduced-height SDBs because SDBs are his major breeding project. His first two MDB introductions, 'Cinnamon Apples' and 'Spot of Tea', won the Caparne-Welch Medal, and both are related tans with prominent red-brown falls spots. Both of these grew well for me in Mississippi, perhaps because they were

'Beetlejuice' is a tiny plicata with a distinct pattern of lines in the area where the *pumila* spot would be, as well as the normal plicata pattern.

'Water Goblins' has tiny flowers born on plants with narrow leaves.

selected in the similarly warm and unpredictable climate of Oklahoma. Paul's SDB plicatas are legion, and his MDBs are no less. These include traditional plicatas 'Stripe Three' and 'Be Brief', as well as "*pumila*-spot-type plicatas," 'Cute as a Button', and 'Beetlejuice'. Glaciatas are the nonmarked whites and creams that fall out of plicata breeding. Paul introduced three outstanding ones—the appropriately named pure-white 'Invisible', cream-and-lemon 'Dollop of Cream', and 'Pearly Whites', sparkling white with orange beards. Two fine dark MDBs are the wide and red-bearded 'Chemistry' and the dark-blue/violet 'Black Olive'. One of the nicest formed of the black MDBs is 'Tingle', cream with a strong fall spot of lemon. Paul said that the first time he saw this flower, he had a tingle too. I see why; it's a great plant. Paul's new introductions, 'Water Goblins' and its sibling 'Twinkle Little Star', are very reduced SDBs, echoing the pumilas of the past with smaller foliage and dense clumps.

Keith Keppel's venture into the MDBs was originally derived mostly from small segregates from SDB breeding, but since then he has line-bred from these varieties. 'Fission Chips' was Keith's first, an incredibly bright orange with full form. It won Keith his first Caparne-Welch Medal. Using 'Fission Chips' as a base, Keith produced 'Icon', a peachy orange with dark fall spot, and from 'Icon' came the more intensely colored 'Mini Series'. Keith's latest creation in this line is the brilliant 'Decibelle', a screaming orange with wide form. Others from Keith's breeding include the ruffled pale-blue 'Rivulet', and 'Brevity', dusky pink with deeper-pink beard.

Don and Ginny Spoon garden in Virginia and have done some significant work in MDBs that has netted them several Caparne-Welch Medals. 'Trimmed Velvet' is dark and looks like the typical SDB dropout. It also is a regular rebloomer. 'Shy' is one of my favorites. It is a tiny white with a beautiful turquoise spot on the falls. The pure-white 'White Ice' is a surprise clean white, a cross between two dark irises. 'Kayla's Song' is a cross of one of those near-sterile SDB × *pumila* hybrids crossed back to an SDB. It is a very in-class, nice neglecta with a rosy blush. Ginny's 'Sapphire Jubilee' is a

well-formed blue with a spot on the falls. It is a prolific grower and reblooms.

Lee Walker is best known for his work with spurias and Japanese irises but became fascinated with the MDBs and started to breed them. 'Short Note' is a cute, small white with wider petals than most. His 'Fire Opal Orange' is appropriately named—a clump of this iris makes a vivid impact. Lee's work with MDB plicatas has been outstanding, and his 'Teacup Sonata' is an unusual brown plicata on a cream ground.

OPPOSITE PAGE, TOP TO BOTTOM The tiny pink with purple spot 'Keep Off' makes a stunning clump.

The subtle 'Cute as a Button' has rounded petals and an unusual pattern.

'Elf Esteem' has a spot with a strong split that adds distinction.

The bright peach with spot 'Icon'

TOP LEFT AND RIGHT The newest of the Keppel MDBs, 'Decibelle'

The ruffled clear-blue 'Rivulet'

MIDDLE LEFT AND RIGHT 'Shy' is a cute white with a thumbprint of turquoise blue.

'Fire Opal Orange' is a bright color on a short stalk.

BOTTOM 'Teacup Sonata' is one of the rare brown plicata MDBs.

Thomas Johnson breeds primarily TBs and SDBs but has made some outstanding contributions to the MDBs as well. From selfing Black's 'Chemistry' came 'Keeno', a bright but dark purple with a red beard, which went on to win the Caparne-Welch Medal. His very dark hybrid 'Kay' honors an aunt whose favorite color is black. One of my favorites is Thomas's 'Alas', clean white with a neat blot of navy blue. Thomas's 'Circa' is a small and tidy white plant with a good blue spot. 'Tiny Clown' is a bright rose-orchid with an even-brighter red beard that just screams "cute!" One of the coolest new MDBs is Thomas's 'Ribbit', a wide and well-formed cream with a prominent green spot and infusions into the standards. It is one of the few new introductions that I bought two of.

We all know the Schreiner family from their huge catalog of gorgeous huge TBs, but you may not know that the next generation of the Schreiner clan, Ben Schreiner, has been quietly creating some gorgeous MDBs that are selling out each year. My favorite of Ben's is 'Pure Juice', in a brilliant shade of orange with a collection of purple lines around the beard, and its companion in

TOP 'Kay' is an exceptionally dark MDB, nearing black.

BOTTOM The cute little MDB 'Ribbit' has outstanding width of petal and a cool green-lemon color.

TOP Boldly colored 'Boggle' is hard to ignore!

BOTTOM 'Pretty Match' is one of the rare reddish amoenas.

yellow with purple lines, called 'Boggle'. These are two irises that will remain choice for years. Several strong bicolors are of note: 'Wait for Me', a very wide formed ivory with a bold thumbprint of purple veins; 'Pretty Match', a near-red amoena; and 'Bitty Beauty', a tiny, dark-navy-blue amoena. In offshoots of the tangerine bearded family, 'Cubbie' offers flowers of beige pink with striking blue beards, whereas 'Small Punch' recalls those Hawaiian punch colors of our youth. Ben is young, but it is clear that he has the gift of hybridizing the small irises, and I expect big things for the future.

TOP 'Small Punch' has those colors we associate with Hawaiian Punch.

BOTTOM 'Pure Juice' has a brilliant orange color with "whiskers" of purple on either side of the beard.

Old Favorites

'Bee Wings' (A. Brown). What a great name! A yellow with a big spot on the falls in that shade of brown black like a bee. A very vigorous plant that covers itself with bloom. My nine-year-old self loved this flower, and it still grows in my garden fifty-eight years later!

'Angel Eyes' (Jones). This was another favorite from my childhood but has been lost along the way. I'm hoping this will show up one day again. A white with a turquoise-blue spot on the falls. Very neat and a tremendous form advancement in its day.

'Red at Last' (Mahood). This one is on the cusp of the SDB class heightwise but has the requisite tiny flower and no branching characteristic of the MDBs. And this is a very respectable little red. After Kelly Norris raved about it in his book, it was one I bought and now cherish too.

'Marmot' (Simonson). I grew this as a kid in Massachusetts, and it is still here many years later. Although the known parts of the pedigree all are pumilas, it has a bit more heft and the flowers are much wider and elegantly formed. It is a lavender blue with a deeper spot.

'Orchid Flair' and 'Dream Stuff' (Mahood). Leona Mahood specialized in these orchid shades that stem from the small *pumila* 'Cretica', but with much-improved form. 'Orchid Flair' and 'Dream Stuff' are two of my childhood favorites. Both are a pleasing shade of orchid.

'Pixie Pirate' (Willott). A blue-purple or navy-blue self with really good form and excellent plant habits, bordering on a weed!

'Heart's Content' (Welch). My favorite of all of Walter's. A very clean and contrasted, almost black amoena. I have been trying to find this one again.

New Favorites

'Alas' (Johnson). This is on the top size for the class but is such an exuberant plant that it is one of my favorites. This iris goes back to the Hager classic 'Self Evident', and this is a much-improved version of this classic.

'Elf Esteem' (Black). A cute little cream white with a prominent purple spot, with a wedge taken out of the bottom of the spot. A contrasted light-blue beard sets off the whole affair.

'Beetlejuice' (Black). A neat, small, rosy-purple plicata with extra plicata marks next to the beard, giving a slight impression of a *pumila* spot. Makes neat, low clumps.

'Oh Grow Up' (Miller). Lynda picks out the best names! This is a cute little variegata in more rose shades than is typical for the MDB class. It is tiny too.

'Dollop of Cream' (Black). Although this is not a showy flower, a subtle cream with lemon highlights, it has a perfection of form to which other MDBs should aspire. A good vigorous grower that makes a pretty clump.

'Small Token' (Miller). What a cute little fellow! To me this is the best red dwarf iris on the market. The foliage is short and narrow.

'Tiny Titan' (Aitken). A beautiful, bright-orange self. This one really glows in the spring garden. Here in the often gloomy and rainy Oregon spring, it is a welcome color relief.

'Pure Juice' (Schreiner). This is an absolutely brilliant orange that somehow seems intensified by an area of broad purple cat whiskers around the beard. The petals are wide and lightly ruffled. I have spread its pollen around to every likely other MDB with tangerine factors in my yard, and the seedlings have been wonderful.

'Ribbit' (Johnson). When I first saw this bloom in the hybridizer's seedling patch, I really wanted this plant. It has some of the widest petals of any MDB, and the colors are a soft greenish lemon, set off by pastel-blue beards. I bought two of these when I could, and have used it as a parent.

REFERENCES

Norris, K. D. *A Guide to Bearded Irises: Cultivating the Rainbow*. Portland, OR: Timber, 2012.

Randolph, L. F., and J. Mitra. "Karyotypes of *I. pumila* and Related Species." *American Journal of Botany* 46, no. 2 (1959): 93–102.

Warburton, B. "Featuring *Iris pumila*." *Bulletin of the American Iris Society* 189 (1968):102–104.

3

Standard Dwarf Bearded Irises

The standard dwarf bearded irises (SDBs) are quite a horticultural miracle. Even though none were released to the market before the pioneering work of Cook and Douglas in the early 1950s, they are now second only to TBs in popularity and number of new varieties on the market. It truly is a miracle to see a class of iris created de novo and so take the world by storm in my lifetime. Part of this popularity has to do with the form, 8–16 inches tall with a mass of about 3-inch-diameter flowers that rise just above the foliage. They are showstoppers in bloom. Because of hybrid vigor, they grow easily in any drained soil and are much more hardy and vigorous than the TBs, and useful in more situations in the border. Best yet, they come in all colors from white to black and in all kinds of exotic patterns. What's not to like?

It was fortunate that when Paul Cook was crossing the dwarf species to TBs in an effort to create bluer TBs (Cook 1950), he crossed TBs with *I. pumila*. Paul had obtained seeds of an Austrian strain of *pumila* from Bob Schreiner, and Paul crossed these, creating a strain of even-bluer pumilas for his crossing to the TBs. TB irises of that time were smaller flowered than the TBs of today, and this fortuitous combination of TBs of that age with Paul's improved pumilas gave rise to a group of irises from the mainly 8–16-inch-tall height range, and beautifully proportioned. Paul named the white with green spot 'Green Spot', the pale yellow 'Baria', and the clear blue 'Fairy Flax'. All three of these irises proved to be wonderful breeders, and scarcely an SDB of today doesn't share its roots with one of these progenitors. The crossing of *pumila* with TBs came about through Paul sending pollen of *pumila* to Geddes Douglas in Tennessee, and Geddes sending pollen of TBs to Paul in Indiana. Geddes (Douglas 1954) made lots of crosses using pumilas and, luckily for us, introduced a whole bunch of them, including members of big families

A clump of an SDB shows just how floriferous these irises are.

from the great blue TB 'Helen McGregor' × Cook pumilas. These introductions, combined with the Cook varieties, gave early SDB breeders some wonderful genetic material. Indeed, many of the F1 TB × *pumila* crosses were horrors and resulted in compost piles full of castoffs. Chief problems were awkward flowers, foliage too big, and flowers down in the foliage. Even today, SDB breeders battle these last two problems. Geddes coined the term "lilliput" for the SDBs (a play on the tiny people from *Gulliver's Travels*), and it is a pity that name was not chosen for the class. Explaining to a novice why we call some miniature dwarfs and others standard dwarfs is a perennial problem.

Unlike many of the irises of this size range, the SDBs are fully fertile. Genetically they are amphidiploids, having two sets of twelve chromosomes from the TB side of the pedigree and two sets of eight from the *pumila* side. Because each chromosome has a partner, meiosis is regular and the SDBs are very fertile, although many are pollen shy. If SDBs are crossed to other SDBs, the progeny are fairly consistent in occupying the 8–16-inch height range. Hybridizers were concerned that this stable condition—two diploid genomes that didn't pair—wouldn't allow for recovery of recessives so that we might get yellows, purples, and dirty whites, much like the old chamaeiris, but not recover interesting recessives, since one parent or the other would have dominants that block the expression of the recessive. Fortunately, both the TBs and the pumilas that went into the SDBs were much more genetically variable. In fact, one of the first triumphs of the early TB × *pumila* crossing was Dorothy Dennis's production of the first SDB plicata 'Dale Dennis', because the little *pumila* from Crete, 'Cretica', had two copies of the plicata recessive all-white gene. Soon every breeder was spreading 'Cretica' on TB plicatas and generating families of plicata SDBs. Similarly, the *pumila* 'Barium Gold' and other pumilas with strong yellow beards proved to be the gateway for bringing the tangerine factors into the SDBs

The *pumila* parent controls the color of progeny in unusual ways. In crosses of *pumila* to TB blues, the TB blue is inhibited, but it does not inhibit its own blue. Thus, the SDB blue and purple color comes from the *pumila* parent in most cases. The intensified color derived from *aphylla*, such as in the TB blacks, does come through partially and resulted in muted gold and purple blends such as 'Blueberry Muffins'. In contrast, *pumila* carotenoids (yellows) are restricted to the beard, but they have a yellow flavone present in high concentrations in the spot. When yellow flavones combine with the anthocyanin, we get a fairly good green color, probably the best in any of the bearded irises. In other irises, greens are a combination of a little anthocyanin overlying a pale-yellow layer. This results in a muddier green.

Another contribution of the *pumila* parent is the spot factor. Most pumilas have a darker spot of color at the base of the beard, and this trait is a dominant one. Indeed, it was difficult for breeders to get self-colored SDBs early in the history of the SDBs. However, these spot patterns are some of the most beautiful in the genus; bold spots of dark purple on gold and dark navy on white verge on gaudy but are so effective in the landscape.

Garden Uses and Culture

SDBs may be used in the garden in almost infinite number of ways, and a number of these are discussed in chapter 7. Because of their vigor, they can be used in the foreground of the perennial border. To keep the SDBs happy, the garden simply needs to ensure that they are not covered up by their border companions. In the rock garden, they are amazing bright spots of color, and in my opinion they have been too little used in that setting. SDBs look great around rocks and add bright spots of color to what can be a drab rock garden.

Because of their smaller size, spot gardens or gardens in small dooryard beds are perfect locations for SDBs. In fact, all medians are good in these spots, but the high density of bloom and shorter rhizomes make SDBs an especially good choice. I have a bed that contains all the dwarf and median classes, and it is a center of interest for a couple of months.

Kinds of Crosses that Generate SDBs

TB × pumila. This sort of cross was behind virtually all of our first SDBs. However, few of these primary crosses are being done today. The most-recent examples of introduced TB × *pumila* seedling that I can recall are Maybelle Wright's 'Wee Ruffles'. which is a seedling from her BB 'Miss Ruffles' and Willott's 'Mr. Roberts' that combines TBs with *pumila*. With all the advances in TBs and BBs since the 1940s, some new crosses of this type are justified. Certainly, factors for lace, dominant amoenas, modern luminatas, and pinks all are areas where new crosses could benefit the SDB gene pool. It was found early on that not all pumilas were created equally in producing high-quality SDBs, and certain clones such Welch H503 and its sibling, 'Aril Morn', were useful. Welch H503 was one of the clones that almost always made pretty progeny. Unfortunately, most of these good-breeding *pumila* clones are no longer available.

SDB × SDB. Almost all the most recent introductions involve crossing existing SDBs with each other. Other than the few small segregates that are MDB size, the progeny are amazingly uniform SDBs.

IB × SDB. Bee Warburton described this as the "squeeze cross," trying to get more of the genes from the TB side of the pedigree into the SDB gene pool. Most of the crosses of this type to date involved tangerine-factored IBs × tangerine-factored SDBs. Early crosses involved the tiny IB 'Lilipinkput' crossed to the Roberts or Brown early-generation SDB pinks. Bee herself crossed her clear pink IB 'Sweetie' with SDBs to obtain her pink SDB 'Betsy Boo'. Because the IBs often contain traits from the TBs that we wish to have in the SDBs, the IB × SDB cross might be an easier approach to bringing these characters into the SDBs than by direct TB × *pumila* crosses.

History of SDBs

Paul Cook had made a few crosses of TBs × *pumila*, including a cross to the TB 'San Francisco', which resulted in a seedling used by Walter Welch and other dwarf breeders. However, it was a cross of blue and yellow pumilas to his blue TB line that shook both Paul and the rest of the horticultural world (Cook 1950). As mentioned, Paul introduced three iconic SDBs from these crosses: 'Green Spot', white with a very green spot on the falls; 'Fairy Flax', a true blue with a deeper spot; and 'Baria', a clear lemon. 'Brite', a cream yellow, was introduced several years later. Paul's first three introductions were heavily used by other breeders, and one of them is behind a majority of the SDBs and IBs on the market today. That's quite a legacy.

The crosses between pumilas and TBs were facilitated by having Geddes Douglas send TB pollen to Paul, and Paul sending *pumila* pollen to Geddes (Douglas 1954). Douglas dubbed his progeny "lilliputs," and one of them was actually named 'Lilliput'. The cross of the TB 'Helen McGregor' × *pumila* was a magic one, and he named the blue selfs 'Small Wonder' and 'Helen's

'Green Spot' was one of the first SDBs introduced and is behind many of the present-day SDBs.

Child' and the blues with deeper spots 'Lilliput' and 'Tinkerbell'. Geddes added the strong group of red violets from 'Minnie Colquitt' × *pumila* that includes 'Jack o' Hearts' and 'Garnet Treasure'. 'Pigmy Gold', from the cross of the short tall orange-yellow 'Orange Glow' × *pumila*, was the first of these SDBs to show what a contribution having the yellows from the TBs brought into the SDBs. Up to that point, other than the highly sterile *I. arenaria* hybrids, only relatively light yellows were available in the dwarfs.

Two siblings to 'Pigmy Gold' proved to be important to the further breeding of the SDBs. A sibling nicknamed "Wee One" was a 4-inch-tall yellow and, when crossed to the TB 'Pink Formal', produced the small IB 'Lillipinkput', which was a very small IB and a player in the development of pink SDBs. The other sibling, 'Little Rosy Wings', turned out to be an outstanding parent. Although the early SDBs were often pollen shy, 'Little Rosy Wings' has abundant and potent pollen. Geddes seemed to be aware that what Paul and he had created was a new class of irises, and he introduced a large variety of irises from a diverse pedigree for use by other hybridizers. Like the Cook SDBs, the Douglas ones, especially the blue 'Tinkerbell', with a deeper spot, and the red-purples 'Garnet Treasure' and 'Little Rosy Wings', proved to be excellent parents for SDBs.

The top award for SDBs, the Cook-Douglas Medal, was appropriately named after these groundbreaking hybridizers. Both of them also won the award named for them.

Because of the large number of hybridizers and the staggering number of SDBs introduced each year (second only to the TBs), I have organized this section by color rather than by hybridizer.

It is a bit strange that pure-white SDBs would be so rare. Early in the development of the SDBs, we had a number of good white cultivars, including Welch's Cook-Douglas Award–winning 'Lilli-White', which is a cross of white chamaeiris types with SDBs. Alta Brown's 'Snow Elf' was a breakthrough in having wider petals and the beginning of what you might call ruffling. Some people would consider Bennett Jones's 'Cotton Blossom' more cream than white, much like the flower of cotton, although in the landscape it looks white. 'Cotton Blossom' was a revolution in form, and its popularity

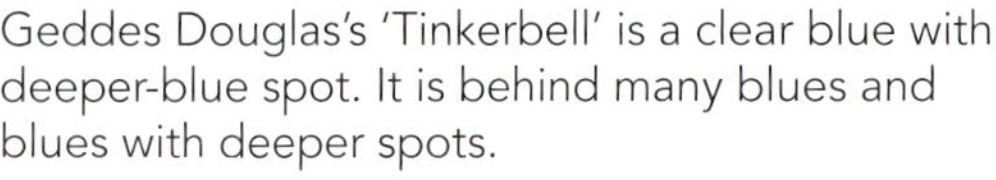

Geddes Douglas's 'Tinkerbell' is a clear blue with deeper-blue spot. It is behind many blues and blues with deeper spots.

'Bluebeard's Ghost' was a major advancement in blue-bearded whites.

was so great it won the Cook-Douglas Medal by a landslide. It has turned out to be a marvelous parent for a wide range of colors. More recently, Jane Ritchie's 'Pure Allure' was a major break in terms of form and was also a very good grower; Keppel's 'Zero' is a more ruffled seedling of 'Pure Allure'. Glaciatas can also give a pure-white effect without any blue influence. Paul Black's 'Sparkling White' is an outstanding example, with beautiful ruffling that completes the picture.

The quest for a white with a strong-blue beard was a long one, although some intermediate steps along the way were interesting too. Dyer's 'Serenity Prayer' was a major break in a cream with small yellow flushes and a strong-blue beard. It comes from crosses of blue-bearded yellows and blues with blue beards. Paul Black's 'Bluebeard's Ghost' took it all the way to white with a blue beard, though. It is one of the few SDBs for which I cast a vote for the Dykes Medal, because it was such a startling advance in color, and a wonderful plant.

Whites with blue spots are one of the most popular patterns in the SDBs, and one that has seen lots of improvements over the years. This is one of the few types of SDBs that have their origin in crosses of chamaeiris with SDBs. Randolph's 'Bright Delight' and Warburton's 'Elisa Bee' were two among the first group of these hybrids that would be the progenitors for this color class, while also cursing them with many two-budded varieties because of chamaeiris in the background. Lynn Markham's 'Boo', derived directly from 'Elisa Bee', is a major advance both in form and contrast. It remained a favorite for many years. Joe Gatty worked this line heavily, and his 'Wink' and Cook-Douglas Medal winner 'Starry Eyed' were important parents. Bennett Jones introduced the amazing 'Blue Pools', which had a more refined form. Paul Black's 'Tu Tu Turquoise' approached turquoise blue in the spot color. More-recent and bolder blue spots can be found on Black's 'Open Your Eyes' and Spoon's 'Huckleberries', which are not only contrasted but beautifully formed as well.

These blue-spotted SDBs lead to even more contrasted versions, some even approaching the white with black spot. Paul Black's 'Puddy Tat' and 'Riveting' and Thomas Johnson's 'Stop and Stare' offer some of the darkest of these dark-spotted SDBs. I'm sure it won't be long before black spots occur in these lines.

'Tu Tu Turquoise' has an unusual turquoise-blue coloring.

'Huckleberries' has white flowers with a strong-navy-blue spot.

Yellow SDBs include some of our early winners and, because of their bright color, are excellent in the garden as strong accents. Bee Warburton introduced two of these early classics. The bold chrome-yellow 'Brassie' and the gold 'Golden Fair' both were from direct TB × *pumila* crosses and were much used as parents for these colors and others. Early on, an unexpected development took place in that crosses of pumilas to some TBs resulted not just in yellows but yellows with blue beards, a color combination not even seen in TBs of that age. Both 'Zing' and 'Blueberry Muffins' had a tawny overtone to the yellow, but the beards were strongly blue. Bee Warburton spent several generations trying to eliminate the tawny in the yellow, resulting in 'Stockholm', clear yellow with strong-blue beards and named for the colors of the Swedish flag. Weiler's 'Little Blue Eyes' is a strong rebloomer and has a clean separation of blue from the yellow. Blues with yellow beards are still being produced. Of the newer ones, Paul Black's 'Experiment' has outstanding contrast between the beard and yellow petals, whereas Keppel's 'Satin Accent' and 'Squirt' are more-pastel cream-and-yellow blends with violet beards. Some of the best new yellows (without blue beards) are glaciatas: Black's 'Blissful' (a creamy yellow with bright orange beard) and 'Lust for Lemon' (a bold and bright lemon) and Johnson's exceptionally bright-gold 'Full Alert' are some of the most exciting.

Variegatas have come easily in SDBs because both the purple spot from *pumila* and the yellow carotenoids from the TBs are dominant. Combining them generates variegatas. These variegatas vary from pale lemons with brown spots to brilliant gold with red-brown falls. One of the early popular variegatas is Alta Brown's appropriately named 'Wow', with chrome-yellow standards and dark-red falls. More recent are Johnson's 'Ultimate', in yellow with a well-defined near-black spot edged in yellow on the falls. A more pastel but equally bright example is Black's 'Zooboomafoo', with stunning orange beards that set the flower on fire. Johnson's 'Searing Embers' combines wonderful wide petals and rounded form with a bold variegata pattern and burnt-orange beards, whereas Black's 'Debonair Bear' is a more pastel cream-and-grape-jelly combo. Variegatas of all types are great garden plants because they have color and pattern that really carries.

Greens have taken two paths in the SDBs, one as advancements in the classic 'Green Spot'

'Squirt' is one of many wonderful blue-bearded yellow SDBs.

The marvelously formed glaciata 'Blissful'

coloration of white flowers with prominent green spots, and the other where the entire flower is green. In the SDBs, the combination of yellow flavones from the *pumila* parent and blue anthocyanin can mix in the vacuoles and make a surprisingly green color. It is one of the few situations where blue + yellow = green, not mud! Early advancements in the green-spotted types were Mildred Brizendine's 'Joy Bringer' and Benson's 'Just So'. 'Dedicated' is a bit more of a lemon yellow and has bright-orange beards, whereas Sutton's 'Little Sighs' verges on a green bitone with a strong spot and colors spilling into the standards. Greens with no spot are rarer. Bennett Jones's 'Kentucky Bluegrass' was a big advance in green selfs, and the prominent blue beard set off the green color of the petals. Ritchie's 'Guacamole' is the closest to green in a self-colored flower that I have bloomed; it looks like a slightly more yellow version of its dip namesake.

TOP 'Zooboomafoo' is a bright variegata.

BOTTOM 'Debonair Bear' has an interesting spot of plum on the falls.

TOP 'Little Sighs' is a green in the tradition of 'Green Spot' but with a blue beard.

BOTTOM 'Guacamole' is a pastel green echoing the colors of the famous avocado dip.

After the wonderful start at blue that the Douglas series from 'Helen McGregor' × *pumila* and Cook's very blue 'Fairy Flax' provided, a number of the early blues paved the way toward truer blues. Bee Warburton's 'Blue Denim' was one of the bluest of the early self blues, although it had the texture veining characteristic of its TB parent, 'Great Lakes'. Alta Brown's 'Sky Baby' combined her white SDB 'Snow Elf' with blue 'Fairy Flax' and had the blue color of 'Fairy Flax', but in a broader form and a better grower. Bee pursued the path to truer-blue SDBs with her 'Dear Love', a direct cross of 'Blue Denim' and 'Fairy Flax'. Bee felt that she had achieved her truest blue in 'Truly'. Further progress in blues seemed to center on the form of the blues rather than approaching true blue. MayBelle Wright's 'Blue Trinket' and 'Wee Ruffles' are from a cross of the BB 'Miss Ruffles' and the *pumila* 'Wee Blue', and they inherited the ruffled form of the BB parent. These were used by others to put form in the SDBs, including Carol Lankow's 'Seaworthy', which combines the well-formed 'Cotton Blossom' with 'Blue Trinket'. Warburton's 'Bay Ruffles' represented a big advance in terms of form in the blues that descend from her blue lines outcrossed to the well-formed 'Crystal Bubbles'. These improved forms continue into more-recent cultivars such as Johnson's 'Clear Blue Sky' and 'Clear Blue Water'. Although the first blue SDBs were light to medium shades, darker shades such as Jones's wonderful 'Rain Dance' and 'True Navy' and more-turquoise flowers such as Black's 'Bombay Sapphire' expanded the range of blue SDBs.

'Tyrian Treasure' is a modern example of the red spot on blues.

'Tinkerbell' was the first SDB blue with a big, bold fall spot of darker blue. Subsequent SDBs followed this pattern, such as Hoffmeister's 'Tres Jolie', but other unique color combos such as Alta Brown's 'Red Heart', a blue with red spot, gave a completely different combination of colors. Both sorts of paths have been followed in more-recent introductions, with Black's 'Devoted' and 'Beyond the Sky', Sutton's 'Tyrian Treasure', and Johnson's 'Prego' representing extremes of the blue red spot theme. Johnson's 'Oh Canada', 'Yodel', and 'Wowzie' represent the blue violet with deeper spot so well. Sutton's 'Small Voice' represents the ultimate form in these spotted navy-blue SDBs, with falls so wide they touch.

One of the patterns unique to SDBs is the blues with spots or infusions of green on the falls. Early examples include Goett's 'Fran Jennings', Peg Edwards's 'Jealous Belle' (which she nicknamed Jelly Belly!!), and Moldovan's 'Blue Martini'. Warburton's 'Sea Change' and Miller's 'Sea Monster' brought this pattern into a more refined form. More-recent examples of this class, appropriately named Tasco's 'Blue Oasis' and Black's 'Green Oasis', have great combinations of blue and green coloration. It's a very cool look and best for close-up inspection. Paul Black's newest ones in this pattern, 'Sky and Meadow' and 'Turtle Tango', take the pattern to an extreme with blue standards and fully green falls.

Reverse amoenas and bitones were patterns more difficult to achieve in the SDBs. Bee Warburton used a *pumila* seedling with a darker flush of blue in the standards and the slight reverse amoena TB 'Blue Angel Wings' to create a line of blue reverse amoenas, leading to 'Sky and Snow' and its seedling 'Gentle Sky'. Despite their popularity, there have been no recent reverse amoenas to my knowledge. There have been several reverse bicolor where the flower has yellow as well as the darker standards, including Spoon's 'Muppet' and brighter 'Cookie Monster', and most recently a pair from Bob Skaggs's boldly colored 'Psycheldelic Dreams' and more pastel 'Reverse Reverse'. These purple-over-yellow combinations are very effective combinations in the garden and rival the TBs in these same colors and patterns.

TOP 'Yodel' is an intense blue violet with a shocking dark spot.

BOTTOM 'Small Voice' has extremely wide petals, with the falls touching at the hafts, and an intense navy coloring.

TOP 'Blue Oasis' is a pastel blue with green highlights.

BOTTOM 'Sky and Meadow' has clear blue standards and green falls.

Reds are difficult in every class of bearded iris. Red SDBs have been available from almost the beginning of the class with Douglas's 'Little Rosy Wings' and 'Garnet Treasure'. Bennett Jones's 'Cherry Garden' was a vast improvement by crossing the outstanding TB red 'Captain Gallant' with a reddish *pumila*. Best yet, 'Cherry Garden' proved to be an excellent parent. The cross of 'Cherry Garden' with Hager's red-violet bitone 'Regards' resulted in the well-formed and redder 'Rangerette' for Melba Hamblen. Carol Lankow's 'Jeweler's Art' represented a significant upgrade in red color, although it comes from lines that are related to other SDBs. It has a brilliance that is hard to describe. Others, such as Don Spoon's 'Red Rabbit', involve 'Jeweler's Art' as a parent. Black's 'Mordor' and Marky Smith's 'Dragonet' represent a return to that red-black coloration that we haven't seen for thirty years in a new introduction.

TOP 'Psychedelic Dream' is a greenish yellow with strong purple infusions into the standards.

BOTTOM 'Mordor' is an exceptionally dark red.

Plicatas were a surprise in the SDBs. The experts had deemed them impossible because they believed *pumila* lacked the genes that would allow expression of the plicata pattern. Dorothy Dennis's production of the stitched purple-on-white plicata 'Dale Dennis', from using the tiny purple 'Cretica' onto the TB plicata 'Mariposa Mia', proved that this was not true. 'Cretica' actually carries the glaciata gene and gives about one-sixth plicatas when crossed to them. Others used 'Cretica' to produce a range of plicata types, although 'Cretica'-derived SDB plicatas have both poor form and substance. A major break occurred in the brown bitone 'Knotty Pine' of Jack Goett's. Jack used a 'Cretica' seedling of Dorothy Dennis's on the TB plicata 'Minnie Colquitt'. 'Knotty Pine' had good form and substance and, when Jack crossed it to existing SDB plicatas, it produced plicatas of much-better form, including the well-marked purple-stitched 'Circlette' and the minimally marked 'Doll Apron', the name a play on the famous TB plicata 'Tea Apron' with the same pattern. A major break in plicatas was Paul Black's 'Chubby Cheeks', a cross of plicatas to the cream 'Soft Air'. 'Chubby Cheeks' is a pastel lavender plicata on white with an almost gauze-like overlay that causes the plicata markings to appear softer; the form was an amazing advance over its predecessors. Not surprisingly, 'Cubby Cheeks' became the go-to parent both for plicatas and form. Its descendants are everywhere in the present SDBs. It was another Dykes-worthy SDB.

Although most of the early SDB plicatas were lighter shades of violet, there has been much progress in producing darker plicatas too. Keppel's 'Dark Design' was one of the most dramatic of

this type, and Mike Sutton's 'Spots and Dots', 'Whiteheart', and 'Grapette' are variations on this theme, with bolder or different markings. Johnson's 'Pirate Baby' has unusual, very dark shoulders in addition to the dark-purple plicata marking. Reddish-violet markings have been available early on in the history of SDBs, such as Molly Price's 'Speckled Sprite'. Chapman's 'Ruby Eruption' combines the fine form of 'Chubby Cheeks' with a yellow ground and strong red-violet plicata markings. Johnson's 'Ciao Bella' has a nice edge of red violet and a flower with exceptional form. Some of the plicatas now approach self colors because the patterns are so intense, such as Sutton's 'Compact' and Johnson's 'My Little Friend'.

Most of the early plicatas were on white bases. Warm plicata SDBs came more slowly. Rundlett's 'Pat's Pal' and Goett's 'Tiffy' have yellow base colors and warmer markings, but not startlingly so. The situation has changed completely in the current SDBs, and this includes all the tangerine base colors in apricot, pink, and orange, with plicata markings in blue, reddish, and brown. Marky Smith's 'Mosaic' has led to a whole line of boldly marked plicatas on warm colors, including her 'Extraterrestrial', 'Martian', and 'Venusian' and Johnson's boldly colored 'Alaia'. Another group is tangerine derived but has lighter-yellow or cream base colors, such as Keppel's lovely 'Raspberry Ice' and Johnson's 'Sweet Devotion' and 'Tasty Treat'. All of these have prominent tangerine to red beards.

TOP 'Chubby Cheeks' was a revolution in form for not just plicatas but for all SDBs. It imparted its fine form to numerous progeny.

BOTTOM 'Compact' has almost-solid purple flowers; the plicata markings are so dense.

ABOVE 'Pirate Baby' has intriguing dark "shoulders."

The luminata pattern was a tougher pattern to bring to an acceptable form. Although Ben Hager's minimally marked 'Whim' was the first, it was Bee Warburton's luminata SDBs that really established this pattern. Bee's pursuit of them started with a cross of the luminata-plicata TB 'Love Affair' with 'Cretica', which resulted in a rosy and an orchid-colored full luminata. Bee pursued these lines for many years and finally produced the dark-purple luminata 'Black Star', rosy-violet 'Rosie Lulu', and blue-violet 'Violet Lulu'. The reason for using the Lulu designation is that the luminata allele at the plicata locus is designated *pl-lu*. Now that there were high-quality luminatas available for breeders, progress on this group became more rapid. Perhaps the most perfect of the newer luminata is Paul

TOP 'Raspberry Ice' is a clear raspberry pink.

BOTTOM 'Alaia' has bright-orange standards and falls strongly marked dark red / purple with strong tangerine beards.

TOP The luminata SDB 'My Cher' is a popular Cook-Douglas Medal winner that is proving to be a great parent.

BOTTOM 'Fishnet Stockings' has a minimal luminata markings on its falls.

Black's 'My Cher', a winner of the Cook-Douglas Medal, in a subtle pastel lavender on a white-flushed gold base color and set off by orange beards. Cher was Paul's wonderful dog, and it is a great tribute to a special animal. Two of Hugh Stout's luminatas, 'My Sheila' and 'Fruit on the Bottom', offer further variations on this pattern and ground colors. Paul Black's 'Fishnet Stockings' represents sort of a minimal luminata with sparse markings just on the falls.

Pink SDBs have been one of the bigger challenges for breeders of this class of iris. As for plicatas, it was at first doubted that pinks could even exist in the SDBs because it requires four copies of the *t* (tangerine) gene for expression, and no one was sure this gene existed within *pumila*. A breakthrough occurred, though, when pumilas with strong yellow beards were crossed onto TB pinks, resulting in pinks for hybridizers Alta Brown, Earl Roberts, Grace Guenther, and several others. The quality of these early pinks was not good, mostly because the pink color was not clear, and the form was downright awful. I remember seeing Roberts's 'Lenna M' and thinking it was hideous. Even this twelve-year-old hybridizer wanted no part of it in crossing!

Breeders have looked at ways of fixing these defects by crossing into well-formed SDB carriers of *t*, such as the well-formed cream 'Cotton Blossom'. MayBelle Wright's seedlings from these sorts of crosses were heavily used by Carol Lankow, resulting in the better-formed 'Pipestone'. Niswonger's 'Ballet Slippers' was an important advance from this line of breeding. Pink IBs were often a surer bet for getting an extra copy of the *t* gene into the SDBs, as well as genes for improved form from the TBs. Bee Warburton's 'Betsy Boo' and Roberts's 'Dache Model' were early examples of this type of cross. Perhaps the ultimate of these uses of IBs is Paul Black's 'Portland Pink'. This is a late-blooming SDB with a hot-pink flower of excellent full, ruffled form. This plant adds *aphylla* into the mix too. One of the clearest and best-formed pinks is Johnson's 'Blushing Diamond', which is also a wonderful plant.

More-standard breeding of pinks has still worked well, and many of these have amazing blue beards that the TB breeders would love to see on their pink flowers. Barry Blyth's 'Chanted' was one of the first to show this color combo, and it proved to be an outstanding parent. One

'Blushing Diamond' has one of the best forms and clean colorations of recent SDB pinks.

'Oh Wow' deserves an exclamation point!!! The dark beard contrasts beautifully with the clear-pink petals.

of its outstanding progeny is Niswonger's 'Tickety Boo', with a cleaner pink flower. Progress continues even further with Black's amazing 'Gate to Paradise' and Johnson's 'Oh Wow', with a beard approaching black.

As mentioned, the first pinks were not clear pinks. When Bennett Jones found that his seedlings were going in the direction of apricot and orange rather than the desired pink, he decided it was one of those when-life-gives-you-lemons-you-make-lemonade moments, or, in this case, oranges! He combined several of the Roberts's approaches to apricot and began line breeding. 'Orange Dazzler' is, as the name implies, a brilliant orange and, unlike the Roberts pinks, has very respectable form; in fact, wide parts. Bennett introduced the whole gamut of orange colors from softer ones in 'Desert Orange' and 'Orange Outrage' to darker ones in 'Orange Tiger', a Cook-Douglas Medal winner. The current class of orange SDBs has taken brightness to a new level with Black's 'Carrot Flash', Rick Tasco's rebloomer 'Forever Orange', and Hugh Stout's 'Baby Carrots'. Most of these rely on the Jones orange lines for their color.

Brown is a color that is not that effective as a landscape color but can be intriguing for close-up inspection. There has been a steady stream of good SDB browns. 'Knotty Pine' was an accidental brown, being a cross for plicatas, not browns, but it had both good color and form. Moreover, it was an exceptional parent. Bennett Jones created one of the most spectacular SDB of the 1960s, 'Gingerbread Man', a brown with brilliant-purple beard. Hybridizers were enthused about this flower, and it was used heavily as a parent. It gave not only better browns but a bevy of other colors and patterns. More recently, browns have been more rare, although Bianco's 'Death by Chocolate'; Michele Bersillon's trio of 'Winkin', 'Blinkin', and 'Nod' (great name for a series); and Paul Black's 'Hear No Evil' and 'Earthly Delight' all are browns with improved form over their predecessors.

The dark-purple-to-black colors are some of the best SDBs, even from the beginnings of the class. Warburton's vigorous 'Derring-Do' and the Brizendine's quite-black 'Shine Boy' were early triumphs from first- or second-generation TB × *pumila* crosses. Unlike TB blue, which is inhibited by the *pumila* parent, that dark color derived from

'Baby Carrots' shows incredibly clean orange color and nice form.

'Earthly Delight' is an unusual brown bitone with the falls bordered the color of the standards.

aphylla is not, allowing the blacks to be expressed in the SDBs. Hager's 'Demon', derived from siblings to 'Shine Boy', was the first SDB that truly appeared black. The Sass chamaeiris 'Black Baby' crossed with the red 'Cherry Garden' gave the red-blacks 'Bing Cherry' and 'Placet'. 'Michael Paul', a 'Demon' seedling, although dark purple rather than black, has outstanding form and vigor and won the Cook-Douglas Medal. Lynda Miller's 'Dark Vader' (what a clever name!!!) comes from a cross of the brown 'Abracadabra' and the blended 'Mrs. Nate Rudolph'. More recently, Keppel's series of dark to black SDBs are derived both from 'Dark Vader' and 'Demon' and bring both the depth and form of these parents. 'Dark Matter', 'Devil Baby', and 'Devil's Night' all have exceptional dark color and fine form, although the shades and beards are different in all three. Also outstanding for its depth of color is Paul Black's 'Bad Intentions', which may be the closest to black so far. Paul's 'Matador's Cape' complements the dark petals with a striking red beard. Such a great combo! As in all the SDBs, contrasting beards can offer lots of interest. In the dark SDBs, putting on white beards adds an amazing note of contrast. Paul Black's 'Wish upon a Star' and its seedling, Johnson's 'Pulsator', are fine examples of this unique beard-petal combination.

Reblooming SDBs are some of the most reliable reblooming irises we have, because they will rebloom in cool climates, where rebloom is often difficult to achieve. Dorothy Dennis's 'Twice Blessed', a cream with yellow intensification, was one of the first to show good rebloom even in northern states. It was the first iris I had rebloom when I gardened in Massachusetts. John Weiler worked the reblooming iris lines heavily and even produced almost continuous bloomers such as 'Thrice Blessed' and 'Triplicate'. Monty Byers is best known for his TB space-agers such as 'Thornbird' and 'Mesmerizer'; he did significant work with SDB rebloomers as well. Most of these took the Weiler cultivars another generation or crossed onto unrelated lines. These include 'Baby Boom' (yellow with deeper spots) and 'Cinders' and 'Darkling' (dark violet with deeper spots). A significant break in rebloomers was Chapman's 'Blueberry Tart', a reverse bitone in blue-flushed purple with a striking blue beard. Hybridizers have used 'Blueberry Tart' to produce such great things as Paul Black's 'Repeat the Blues', a clean blue with a deeper-blue beard. Terry Aitken introduced the most amazing repeat bloomer in his 'Fairy Fireworks', a clean plicata that starts blooming

TOP Keith Keppel has introduced many outstanding dark SDBs such as 'Devil's Night'.

BOTTOM 'Fairy Fireworks' is a reliable repeat bloomer, putting up three sets of bloom stalks.

with the SDBs and continues to produce waves of flowers through the TB season. This is considered repeat blooming rather than reblooming because there is no period of nonbloom.

Old Favorites

Probably no other class of median has gone through such dramatic advancement as the SDBs, but a few older ones pull personal heartstrings for me.

'Blueberry Muffins' (Warburton). What a breakthrough this iris was in its day. 'Blueberry Muffins' is a tawny gold with a bit of green intensification on the falls and a startlingly big blue beard. It had what became "Bee's form": domed standards and broad, absolutely flaring falls. Also a great and clever name.

'Boo' (Markham). 'Boo' was a real advance in blue spots on white, and I was lucky enough to see its maiden bloom. Lynn had run out of space in her garden and grew this cross at Bee Warburton's. Its maiden bloom was the day of the regional tour there. It went on to win an AM and was on the Median Iris Society popularity poll for many years. It is behind many of the present-day SDBs in this pattern. In fact, Lynn became known as "Boo's mother" in iris circles.

'Fairy Ballet' (Sarro). I first saw 'Fairy Ballet' growing as a guest plant at Bee Warburton's garden, and later grew it myself. It has orchid standards and falls in a much-deeper shade, with a perfect edge the color of the standards. If this plant had been distributed earlier, it would have won all sorts of awards.

'Little Hiawatha' (Bishop). Polly Bishop was my mentor in the iris world. She grew a large crop of SDB seedlings for several years, using many of the best of the 1960s and '70s. 'Little Hiawatha' came from a most fortuitous cross between two Cook-Douglas Medal winners, 'Blueberry Muffins' × 'Cherry Garden'. It is gold with falls brushed a bright chestnut. The form was a big jump for this class, and it still looks pretty good even compared to the current crop of SDBs.

'Little Hiawatha' a brown bitone with especially wide form for an iris of its age.

'It's a Small World' a delicate white with pink styles.

New Favorites

'Alaia' (Johnson). Oh what a color and pattern! A very vivid, warm plicata with orange standards and cream falls strongly bordered in russet, all set off by a strong-orange beard. Round, ruffled shape and a great grower make for a near-perfect plant. Thomas named this iris for his dog, and it has the same sparkling personality as its namesake. Very fertile, and the seedlings that bloomed were uniformly amazing.

'Blushing Diamond' (Johnson). A clear pink with a white blaze on the falls and marvelous ruffling and broad segments all too rare in pink SDBs. Nicely branched, and it blooms for a long season. Very good increaser too. My only complaint is that I wish it were more fertile, although it's not a mule. I should see its seedlings next spring.

'Fairy Fireworks' (Aitken). Even if this plant didn't repeat-bloom, I would still grow it for its clean white with distinct purple stitching and its fine form. However, repeat this plant does. It starts blooming with the SDBs and then sends up a second set during IB / early TB and a third set during the TB bloom, totaling about six or seven weeks of bloom total. Luckily, 'Fairy Fireworks' passes this trait on to its children.

'Guacamole' (Ritchie). Jayne Ritchie lived in Washington and was a backyard hybridizer, having created quite a few nice medians, including President's Cup winner IB 'Bedtime Story'. 'Guacamole' is a pale green that sort of reminds one of the famous avocado preparation. It is odd for a green SDB in that the green is not confined to the spot. The pedigree is more than a little intriguing because it has plicata and other parents that shouldn't give greens, but here it is. This has been a fun parent.

'It's a Small World' (Black). This is a rather rare SDB; although a plicata, the purple markings are small, confined to the haft. What is striking are the bright-pink styles and hafts topped by a red beard. What a combo! The shape is lovely too—broad and lightly ruffled. This has been a very interesting parent.

'My Cher' (Black). When I moved to Oregon in 2010, Cher was Paul's dog, and Cher decided I was a very special person (of course, I did bring treats when I visited, which may have influenced that opinion). When Paul bloomed this luminata SDB, he wished to name it for Cher, but Roger Nelson had already named a TB 'Cher'. I then suggested he call it 'My Cher' instead because it would also signify the name was for his dog and not the entertainer. Problem solved. 'My Cher' has graced my garden since it was introduced, and its wonderful lavender luminatas please every spring. It has also been a potent parent, and none of its kids are "dogs" either!

'Yodel' (Johnson). This one is rich! The standards are a rich purple, but the falls have a very intense near-black spot, rimmed by the color of the standards. The petals are wide and the falls flare horizontally. A vigorous plant and extremely healthy.

REFERENCES

Cook, P. "Report to Scientific Committee." *Bulletin of the American Iris Society* 119 (1950): 58–59.

Douglas, G. "The Lilliput Story." *Iris Yearbook of the British Iris Society* 1954 (1954): 61–64.

Wright, M. B., and B. Warburton. "Standard Dwarf Bearded." In *World of Irises*. Edited by B. Warburton and M. Hamblen, 156–165. Wichita, KS: American Iris Society, 1978.

4

Intermediate Bearded Irises

Intermediate bearded irises (IBs) are intermediate between the dwarfs and tall bearded both in height (16–27 inches tall) and blooming season. IBs tend to be vigorous and floriferous, having more buds than the dwarf irises. They fill a gap in the iris growing season, allowing for a continuous series of bloom from the earliest miniature dwarf into the BB and TB seasons. Because many current intermediates are hybrids of the SDB and TB irises, they often inherit the unique spot and eyelash patterns of the SDBs with the sophisticated forms and colors of the TBs. Putting all of that all into one flower makes for

A clump of Paul Black's lovely 'Meditation Garden', showing the floriferous nature of IBs a very special plant for gardeners. Gardeners have long appreciated IBs. Linnaeus named the first iris species *Iris germanica* but did not recognize that this purple-bearded iris was a natural hybrid, possibly between two no-longer-extant species (Service 1997), and, because it is no longer a species but a hybrid clone, it should be designated as 'Germanica'. 'Germanica' is sterile, so the plant was spread by the actions of man, who used it to decorate homes and gravesites. It also inherited the vigor and hardiness inherent in its hybrid nature to be grown all over Europe. It made its way to the United States, where virtually everyone's grandmother had a patch of this iris as well. White-flowered versions of this or similar crosses in the wild, some of which are designated as 'Alba' or 'Albicans', are also widely grown. These white forms seem to have been especially cherished in some cultures, and it is thought that Muslims carried these irises throughout their empire to plant on graves (Warburton 1984). Virtually every old garden in the southeastern US had one of these white types growing. Their indestructible nature made them favorites for generations of gardeners.

Today's IBs have that same indestructible nature, but with far-prettier flowers in a range of colors from white to black, and are often conspicuously marked with veins, thumbprints, or other interesting patterns. Because they bloom generously and pose no problem in culture, these are irises that should be grown more widely than they are. They are perfect for home gardeners with limited space or who garden in climates where windy and rainy conditions during bloom season knock down taller TB stalks.

Although the IBs were once considered sterile dead ends, Marky Smith and others have recently shown that many of the modern IBs have a fair degree of fertility, depending on the cultivar. Segregation of traits in these sorts of crosses shows a wide range of sizes and bloom seasons. The resultant plants are classed as IBs or BBs, depending on bloom seasons and flower qualities. In contrast, IBs derived from *I. aphylla* crosses are highly fertile because they contain balanced sets of chromosomes. The Craigs and Paul Black have made notable progress in these lines. Branching on many of the *aphylla* hybrids is almost excessive, with stalks with ten or more buds common.

Garden Uses and Culture

IBs are one iris that I don't mind giving to a less experienced gardener; success is almost ensured if the plants are given sufficient sunlight and good drainage. My mother had two lists of plants: ones that she gave to good gardeners, and a second list "that any fool could grow." IBs made the second list.

Here in Oregon, the IBs start to bloom just as the tulips and daffodils are fading, although when I gardened with them in Massachusetts, they bloomed with the late tulips and offered colors that would complement and cool down the vibrant reds of the tulips and add blue and purple shades to the daffodils. In Oregon the IBs fill in a gap in the perennial bloom season as well, starting as the *Pulmonaria* species and hybrids are fading and before the onset of garden stalwarts such as peonies, columbines, and hardy geraniums, which continue the bloom season. Clumps of IBs distributed throughout the perennial border can produce up to a month of bloom if different cultivars are used. Because they can be had in any color from white to black, they fit into any color scheme.

Like the other small irises, IBs can be used in smaller areas and narrow beds where a bigger iris would look out of place. I have them in a small bed with a mix of all median and dwarf classes together, resulting in a bed with several months of continuous bloom. Because of the vigor of many IB cultivars, they might need to be dug up and divided more often than the TBs or BBs. However, this can be a good problem because you'll have plenty of rhizomes to share with friends and establish new plantings.

Kinds of Crosses That Generate IBs

TB × SDB crosses. Most of the IBs on the market now are from crosses of SDBs with TBs. Because both SDBs and TBs are highly refined flowers, the resultant IB hybrids are themselves often highly refined as well. Before the establishment of the SDB class, crosses of TBs with the so-called chamaeiris dwarfs produced hybrids that were popular with gardeners but lacked the refinement of those from TB × SDB breeding.

Derivatives of *I. aphylla*. *I. aphylla* is a highly branched, short tetraploid species and when crossed to TBs often produces fine IBs. Because the form and substance of *I. aphylla* is much less sophisticated than the SDBs, the IBs involving this species have a wildflower look, especially in F1 hybrids. Advanced generation crosses look more like the other IB hybrids but generally have the branching and stalk typical of *aphylla* rather than the clubbier, tightly branched stalk typical of the TB × SDB hybrids.

Grab bag of other approaches. In the early days of the Median Iris Society, many dwarf species were crossed onto both tetraploid and diploid to see if any of these combinations gave good garden plants or might add new or interesting genes to the TB gene pool. One of the more successful of these was Paul Cook's cross of 'Shining Waters' with a yellow *I. reichenbachii* to give the rather homely bicolor 'Progenitor'. An untrained hybridizer would have tossed out such a flower, but Paul recognized right away that this cross demonstrated a dominant inhibitor of color in the standards. At the IB level, he was able to create 'Kiss Me Kate', a classy white with falls rimmed blue, which won the Sass Award. Now the genes from 'Progenitor' have been used in almost every class of bearded iris, and bicolors and amoenas of all kinds are the result. Earl Roberts used a 'Progenitor' × *pumila* seedling of Paul Cook's crossed with TBs to create his Elfin series of IBs; these are a bit shorter and daintier than those derived from TB × SDB breeding. Several irises were introduced from crosses of *I. suaveolens* (= *mellita*) and *I. attica* crossed onto TBs. Bee Warburton's 'Proper Lemon' and Jack Goett's 'Mellite' were among the best, but all of these were more prone to virus than the IBs from SDB crosses, and it is doubtful that any are extant.

Why Are Most IBs Sterile?

There are three groups of fertile dwarfs and medians: diploids (most MTBs), tetraploids (BBs and tetraploid MTBs), and amphidiploids (SDBs and many MDBs; see discussion in chapter 8). What all these irises have are groups of chromosomes that can pair with each other during meiosis, the formation of pollen and ovules in irises. This pairing of chromosomes is critical for the formation of functional pollen and ovules.

The situation in the IBs is different. They inherit two sets of twelve chromosomes from their TB parent and an odd combination of one set of twelve chromosomes and one set of eight chromosomes from the SDB parent. In the odd combination, four chromosomes from the set of twelve and four chromosomes from the set of eight are able to pair, but the remaining chromosomes do not. These nonpairing chromosomes are either lost or are distributed unevenly to the pollen or ovule cells. My rule of thumb is that whenever there are more chromosomes that pair than don't, at least some fertility can be expected. Pollen formation seems to be more sensitive to these chromosomal problems than the ovules, so I generally use the IBs as pod parents rather than pollen parents. However, several workers have had success with IB pollen, both to other IBs and to SDBs. The progeny in these crosses includes some rather strange segregates: 12-inch dwarfs with huge flowers, tiny flowers on 36-inch-tall stalks, and some nice IBs and BBs.

"Aril-Medians" and "SPEC-X"

Aril irises are not eupogon irises, as are the other irises in this book, but crosses of eupogon irises with various species of the onco, aril, and regelia groups that are under the auspices of the Aril Society International, not the Dwarf Iris or Median Iris Societies. These aril irises tend to be much more difficult to grow than the dwarfs or medians, requiring sharp drainage and a climate with a low-rainfall summer. Crosses of these irises to SDBs chiefly have resulted in plants that are better suited to gardens than arils or aril × TB hybrids, although they find my yard too wet and quickly perish for me as well. These aril × SDB crosses have been nicknamed Aril-Medians, or the shortened form Aril-Meds, but these are not officially accepted terms of the American Iris Society. Their colors and patterns are exotic, and if you live in a less soggy yard than mine, they are definitely worth a try. Luckily, my friends here in Salem grow them well, so I can admire them, but I don't torture them by planting them in my yard!

Some of the hybrids that would fall into the IB class are sometimes registered as SPEC-X (species hybrids) if they look less sophisticated (more of a wildflower look) than the IBs, because they are either first-generation crosses to species or are irises that don't fit any class exactly. Examples of this include the parchment-colored 'Understated', blue with brilliant beard 'Night Mood', near-amoena 'Aphylliated' (the name a pun on its *aphylla* parent), ruffled plicata 'Wild Petticoats', and neglecta 'Date with Destiny'. All of these are fun flowers and well worth growing.

Not all of the bearded SPEC-X hybrids fall in the IB class or are tetraploid. Some, such as Silver's 'Clown Pants' and Edinger's 'Magyar Medley', are

TOP SPEC-X 'Night Mood'

BOTTOM SPEC-X 'Aphylliated'

ABOVE SPEC-X 'Date with Destiny'

from species and MTB cultivars. These are charming plants despite not fitting exactly in any class. It is great that irises such as these can be grown and admired.

History of IBs

Caparne was one of the first dwarf iris breeders (see chapter 2), but he soon became aware that there was a gap between the bloom of dwarfs and TBs. To fill this gap, he began crossing the dwarfs onto the tall bearded of the time and obtained the first artificially produced IBs. To consummate these crosses, Caparne forced TB irises in a greenhouse so they would bloom early enough to cross the dwarfs with the TBs. These crosses worked just as Caparne had predicted, and a new race of irises, the IBs, was born, intermediate in height and season between the dwarfs and TBs. Creamwhite 'Ivorine', blue-purple bicolor 'Prince Victor', and the clean-yellow 'Queen Flavia' were some of Caparne's hybrids. He was in contact with the German firm G&K and sold plants to them. G&K used these and their own hybrids to produce white 'Ingeborg' and rich-blue bicolor 'Walhalla'. These G&K hybrids were quite popular with the gardening public, and several of the Caparne and G&K IBs can still be found in historical iris collections.

Diploid SPEC-X 'Magyar Medley'

It was the Sass brothers, however, who really popularized the IBs, and the American Iris Society rewarded them, naming the medal for best IB for them—the Hans and Jacob Sass Medal. The Sass brothers lived in the cold climate of Nebraska, and the so-called chamaeiris dwarfs were exceptionally hardy. To extend that hardiness into the TBs, crosses were made between the dwarfs and the TB, and IBs of great hardiness were obtained. As a bonus, many also rebloomed, even in the cold climate of Nebraska. The Sass brothers raised thousands from these crosses and chose only eighteen to be introduced. Although these plants were produced in the 1930s and 1940s, they proved very popular and were still common in gardens when I was gardening as a kid in the 1960s. With their hardiness and vigor, I'm betting many are still extant. One of the desires of the Sass brothers was to increase the color range from the white, cream, and purple of the previously available IBs. Among the IB varieties introduced, the white strong rebloomer 'Autumn Queen', the reblooming blue 'Ultra', dark-purple and strong rebloomer 'Eleanor Roosevelt', and the first sort of "green" iris 'Doxa' were among the most enduring. Some of these reblooming IBs were used as parents (although quite infertile ones) to extend the reblooming trait into the TBs. The Sass brothers did not do things on a small scale and eventually got improved tall bearded rebloomers from the breeding of IBs × TBs.

Bob Schreiner was one of the pioneers in intermediate iris breeding during this same time period. A fortuitous late blooming of the blue-purple dwarf 'Marocain' with pollen of the tall bearded 'Swazi' produced several fine intermediates, inspiring a more extensive approach. A more intensive crossing effort with 8,000 IB seedlings resulted in the introduction of several unique IBs: the clearwhite 'Alaska', burnished ruby-red 'Ruby Glow', and probably their most famous, 'Black Hawk'. At the time it was introduced, 'Black Hawk' was one of the darkest irises available in any class. Years later, Bob used SDBs crossed to TBs to create fine intermediates and to bring spot patterns from *I. pumila* into the TBs. His 'Cutie', white with blue-lined falls, and 'Drummer Boy', a similar blue with deep-blue lines, were both Sass Medal winners and remained popular into the 1980s.

I consider Wilma Greenlee the founder of the modern IB. Although she introduced classic TB × chamaeiris IBs before the SDBs were derived, when Paul Cook gave her pollen of his new SDBs to cross to TBs, a whole new type of IB was born. When the white 'Cloud Fluff' and the blue with deeper thumbprint 'Blue Asterisk' bloomed, they represented revolutionarily better IBs. Both of these would be Sass Award winners and were grown for years. One of the rare IB × IB crosses from these first-generation seedlings gave the clear 'First Lilac'. Wilma continued her hybridizing with a series of plicata IBs ('Snow Fleck', 'Glimmer', 'Raspberry Acres', and 'Rocket Flame') and two blends ('Brownie Troupe' and 'Indian Doll'). All are highly rated and long-popular garden irises. In addition to these fine irises, Wilma distributed several seedlings, including an ahead-of-its-time pink/blue bicolor out of *I. balkana* and seedlings from several generations of a cross between the tall bearded pink 'Cherie' and the red-violet *I. pumila* 'Nana', which was used by many to produce pinks in the SDBs and IBs.

Although Alta Brown worked in every dwarf and median class, her IBs were probably the most outstanding. She garnered several Sass Medals for her hybrids. Of course she had her outstanding line of SDBs, and the TBs of her husband, Rex, to use in her breeding, which greatly facilitated this work. She also defied the idea that "the IBs are sterile," and used several IBs in crosses with TBs to produce IBs with more-sophisticated flowers. An early success was the lovely 'Lime Ripples', a greenish-yellow self that went on to win the Sass Award; it remained on the popularity poll for years. Alta used the stable name Arctic for a series of IBs, with the strongly contrasted purple-and-white plicata 'Arctic Fancy' and the velvety red-black 'Arctic Night' being two of the outstanding selections. 'June Prom' was considered the perfect IB when it was introduced, and it still looks quite modern more than forty years after its introduction. It has soft-blue flowers, shaded deeper around the hafts and bottoms of the standards. Alta produced some of the first pink SDBs and a number of pink IBs, including 'Pink Pride' and its seedling from selfing it, 'Pink Reverie', and the more raspberry-toned 'Raspberry Flip'. One of Alta's later introductions, 'Orange Riot', won prizes in Europe because it was an outstanding brilliant orange, when such colors were rare.

Although Bee Warburton's main emphasis was the SDBs, she made major contributions to the development of the IBs as well, developing IBs from the usual TB × SDB route but also from other species. From a cross of the great Cassebeer blue TB 'Blue Whisper' with her blue SDB 'Blue Denim' came the siblings white 'Frosted Cups' and blue 'Dilly Dilly'. This beautiful pair demonstrated what a good IB was: vigorous with perfectly formed flowers and a nearly perfect stalk. Both were childhood favorites of mine. Later Bee produced one of the boldest plicatas in 'Snappie' and one of the most subtle but beautiful irises in 'White Lilacs'. One of her first IBs was 'Berry Parfait', and its name aptly describes the two-toned, luscious berry colors in this flower. However, its flower was way out of proportion for the size of the stalk, and Jack Goett said he "would never speak to her" if she introduced it, because people would love the colors but it would always be a bad example for what proportions should be. She finally did introduce it twelve years after registering it, figuring that by then it could do no damage. Two of her *I. aphylla* seedlings, the maroon-red 'Maroon Caper' and the shining dark-navy-blue 'Annikins', were AM winners and showed the promise of these sorts of crosses in producing fertile IBs. Ironically, Bee was never able to get anything good from either of these irises and gave up this approach. Luckily, others were able to capitalize on these two and produce both IBs and tetraploid MTBs from them.

Earl Roberts was the first president of the Median Iris Society and maintained a test garden for many years in his Indiana garden. Earl obtained a seedling of Paul Cook's, from a 'Progenitor' × *I. pumila* cross, and crossed it onto TBs. He introduced the seedlings from this cross under the stable name Elfin because they were daintier than IBs from TB × SDB crosses. The range of colors was impressive: the olive-green 'Elfin Erin', dark-purple 'Elfin Royale', snow-white 'Elfin Princess', and antique-gold 'Elfin Antique'. Unlike the TB × SDB–derived IBs, Earl's Elfin series had a fair degree of fertility despite having forty-four chromosomes. Earl was the first to develop pink SDBs; these proved to be good parents for IBs too. Pinkish-apricot 'Amber Waves' and pastel-pink bitone 'Cherie Amour' were two selected from this work.

Gordon Plough was best known for his TBs; he made notable advances in dark red / blacks, plicata, yellow amoena, and orange TBs. Gordon grew all the bearded-iris classes, and some of his playing involved crosses of SDBs with TBs and BBs. 'Sing Again' was a popular yellow amoena IB combining his yellow amoena TB 'Sing Along' with SDBs. It won a well-deserved Sass Medal. Two of my favorites of the Plough IB were the siblings 'Dew Point' and 'Tumwater', which combined the blue-with-strong-blue-beard BB 'Blue Miller' with SDBs. 'Dew Point' is a smaller, earlier version of 'Blue Miller', whereas 'Tumwater' was more of a yellow and blue blend with a contrasted blue beard. Gordon also explored tetraploid routes to IBs, resulting in 'Flarette', a navy from *aphylla* breeding, as well as three from dominant amoena breeding—the amoena with a darker belly stripe 'Beebop', the strongly contrasted amoena 'Le Sabre', and the pastel amoena 'Ping Pong'.

Steve Moldovan was one of those cutting-edge hybridizers in the 1960s and 1970s. He introduced irises for Orville Fay and Brother Charles Reckamp—the royalty of TB breeders—and also the Roberts pink SDB varieties. It was only natural to combine these extraordinary TBs with the new pink SDBs to try to create some revolutionary IBs. These included bright-apricot-orange 'Cumquat', pink amoena 'Turtledove', lavender with reddish fall spot 'Rainbow Bridge', and creamy-pink 'Heartstrings'. These hybrids introduced many new combinations and colors to the IB class. Not all of the crosses were between the Roberts SDBs and TBs, though: a cross of Schreiner's dark-purple TB 'Royal Touch' and Bee Warburton's SDB 'Blueberry Muffins' produced 'Aquarius', a pale blue with deeper beard. 'Aquarius' raised eyebrows when it was introduced for the astronomical price of one hundred dollars, which may have delayed its distribution. However, it was certainly worthy of the price, considering its advancement in the class, even though IBs of the day were often introduced in the ten-to-fifteen-dollar range.

Joe Gatty had developed a strong line of SDBs when he lived in New Jersey. A move to California to partner with TB guru Keith Keppel allowed Joe to combine the Keppel TBs with his SDBs, and some wonderful IBs resulted. All of these showed off the improved form from the modern TB parents used. Probably the most widespread of these IBs is the Sass Medal winner 'Early Edition', a clean dark-navy-blue plicata on a clean white ground. For many years it was top of the Median Iris Society popularity poll because it performed well all over the country. 'Vamp', which Joe once described as a "screaming harlot" (Gatty 1985), is a bright flower in iridescent red violet with a deep spot near the beard. Joe definitely raised the bar in terms of IB color and form. Keith carried on Joe's tradition of breeding IBs from the best of his SDB and TB lines. I'm sure Joe would be proud of Keith's achievements. Two of Keith's Sass Medal winners—'Ruby Slippers' and 'Garnet Slippers'—are brilliantly colored maroon red with bright beards, a cross of tangerine-bearded SDBs and red-bearded black TB lines. Both of these irises are great clumps. Keith's 'Dark Triad' combines his near-black SDB with his line of riffled dark purples and is almost as dark as 'Dark Matter'. Keith is "Plicata Man" and used his soft cream 'Soft Word' to create the ultimate IB glaciata, 'Blank Verse'. Keith's IB 'Broken Promise' is the rare broken-color IB, a tan

plicata with the yellow color varying from flower to flower. The sport of this plant lacks all the yellow coloring, revealing a lavender plicata. Keith's most recent IB is the vivid dark plicata 'Group Hug' (and don't we all need one of these).

Hooker Nichols started breeding as a youth and is still at it. His IB introductions are some of his finest. Early successes include the miniature version of the green bitone TB 'Bayberry Candle', named 'Emerald City', and the first of the space-age IBs, 'Hagar's Helmet', a yellow with horns. Hooker and his wife, Bonnie, are doing much to add space-agers to the IB class. My two favorites are also Sass Medal Winners: 'Oklahoma Bandit' and 'Bottled Sunshine'. 'Oklahoma Bandit' is tan with a prominent red-brown spot, sort of "cowboy colors," making for a showy flower. 'Bottled Sunshine' is a seedling of the TB 'Joyce Terry' and brings that pattern of bright-gold standards over white falls with gold borders to the IB class. Hooker might disagree, but I think this is his best hybrid. It never makes a bad flower and is a maniac plant.

Alan Ensminger is the self-proclaimed "Wizard of Odds," known for his broken-colored irises. His IBs are not broken colored, but many are quite lovely. His first triumph is the extremely vigorous blue with deeper-blue beard 'Az Ap'. This strange name is Alan's way of telling others that 'Az Ap' was a miniature of the TB 'Azure Apogee'. 'Az Ap' grows vigorously across the country and won

TOP Clean glaciata IB 'Blank Verse'

BOTTOM The dark IB 'Dark Triad'

ABOVE 'Unbroken Promise' is a sport of the brown erratic plicata 'Broken Promise'.

the Sass Medal. Unfortunately, later this plant became heavily infected with mosaic virus, and the flowers now are almost always marred by darker-blue striations. Fortunately, Alan's other IBs have not showed this tendency. Sass Medal winner 'Blue Eyed Blond', a yellow with striking blue beard, was one of the first to bring this pattern, common in the SDBs, to the IBs. Alan had been experimenting with crossing bright yellows into reds to improve the brightness and redness of the reds. His 'Morning Show' is a good example of such a cross. It obviously impressed American Iris Society convention goers, because it won the President's Cup despite heavy competition from the TBs. Alan developed many "dark top" SDBs and MDBs, and combining them with the Shoop dark-top TBs gave the brown standards and yellow falls 'John'. The American Iris Society gave Alan the Hybridizers Medal for his innovative breeding program.

Terry Aitken, along with his wife, Barbara, runs Aitken's Salmon Creek Nursery in Vancouver Washington, which has promoted dwarf and median irises from its inception. Terry's breeding of IBs has been one of his most successful efforts. Terry used the TB Dykes Medal winner neglecta 'Mystique' in many crosses, and they were wildly successful. Perhaps the greatest of these is the small version of 'Mystique', the IB 'Hellcat'. Form, color, and growth are all superb, and it quickly won a Sass Medal. A cross of Terry's dark TB 'Gyro' (also a 'Mystique' child) crossed with a seedling gave the rich, dark-blue/purple 'Dark Waters'. 'Dark Waters' has both lovely form and an extremely aggressive and healthy plant. It also went on to

TOP One of Hooker Nichols's finest irises is the IB 'Bottled Sunshine'.

BOTTOM Dark-navy-blue 'Dark Waters' is an outstanding performer.

ABOVE 'Jack of Clubs' approaches spectrum black.

win the Sass Medal. One of my favorites of Terry's IBs is the lemon-yellow 'Maui Moonlights'. This combines the improved shape from the SDB 'Cotton Blossom' through the SDB 'Lemon Rings', giving a much more sophisticated flower in the IBs. One of the most exciting new IBs is Terry's 'Jack of Clubs'. Close to true black and with perfect form, it is a wonderful addition to the color range.

Dave Niswonger's work in IBs has produced some solid varieties. His first, 'Honey Glazed', is one of the rare IBs from an SDB × IB cross. The name describes it well—cream standards and light, honey-brown falls. 'Bluebird in Flight' is from his outstanding BB 'Marmalade Skies' but is different in color, a pastel amoena with a bright-orange beard. Dave hit a jackpot when he crossed the Keppel glaciata 'Goddess' with the fat SDB 'Chubby Cheeks', which generated the Sass Medal Winner dark-red/violet plicata 'Prince of Burgundy', as well as the greenish plicata 'Goddess of Green' and the soft-lemon glaciata 'Goddess of Yellow'.

Although George Sutton and son Mike are known for their TB rebloomers and novelty spooned and flounced TB irises, they have also produced a number of wonderful IBs with these characteristics. Deep-navy 'October Storm' has a big flounce on each fall. 'Red Hot Chili' is a bright-red plicata on a bright-lemon ground color. My favorite of the Sutton IBs is the lined plicatas—blue/violet-marked 'Line Drive', red/violet-marked 'Spiked', and white-and-yellow-ground 'Fall Line'. All these are good rebloomers, even in Oregon.

One only has to look at the pedigrees of the IBs from Jim and Vicki Craig to understand the work they put in to produce IBs and other medians through *I. aphylla*. In addition to their own crosses, they used some of Ben Hager's seedlings and named varieties from *aphylla* breeding. All these varieties have great branching and a more modern form than most varieties from similar breeding. These varieties include white 'Departure', white with blue spot on the falls 'Dancing Falls', strong-blue/violet 'Passage', pastel variegata 'Fresh Image', and the blended blue 'Tie Dyed Tyke'.

Larry Lauer's garden is only a ten-minute drive (and just two turns) from mine, so we visit each other's garden and also entertain spring visitors. Although Larry's focus is the TBs, he has introduced quite a few medians as well. 'Lemon Pop' is an amazingly vigorous and brightly colored lemon yellow. Reblooming irises are a specialty of Larry's too, and his IB 'Rust Never Sleeps' is a reliable one. The color is unusual too—pink infused with bronze and a bright-blue beard.

Vibrant 'Red Hot Chili'

Strikingly marked 'Line Drive'

TOP 'Dazzling' is a fine amoena and a great performer.

MIDDLE 'Star in the Night' is well named—the white beards stand out in contrast to the dark-purple petals.

BOTTOM The beautifully formed 'First Lady of Spring'

Paul Black's work with IBs is extensive and includes both the traditional SDB × TB crosses and several *I. aphylla*–derived IBs. One of his first IBs, and still a great plant, is 'Harlow Gold', golden yellow with a small white blaze on the falls. 'Red Zinger' is a clean red IB with excellent growth habits. A planting of these two in my garden in Mississippi was stunning; they set off each other's colors. Many of Paul's IBs have proven to be fertile, and you see his 'Red Zinger' involved in many pedigrees, both IB and otherwise. Paul has a whole stash of Sass Medal winners. 'Nickel', named for a favorite Siberian husky mascot at Mid-America Gardens, is a dark-purple-on-white plicata. Not quite husky colors, but close. Paul even won two Sass Medals from one cross! Both 'Dazzling', a clean amoena with a narrow white edge to the falls, and 'Man's Best Friend', with blue standards and reddish falls, like a larger version of the SDB 'Devoted', its parent, came from the same pod. One of the most striking of Paul's IBs is 'Star in the Night', a dark navy blue with a white-tipped beard that sets off the whole flower. 'Star in the Night' is incredibly vigorous and makes great clumps of blooms. One IB that is hard to ignore is the brilliant-gold 'Brazen Gold', which has exquisite form and coloring and is a killer plant as well. Paul's fertile line of IBs started with 'Alberta Clipper', a clear blue with darker-blue beard, which involves both SDBs and tet MTBs in the pedigree. Lots of wonderful genes there! Paul has made use of it in a number of his breeding lines. 'First Lady of Spring' is a most amazingly ruffled clear white, nearly an MTB in size. Dark-violet amoena 'Casual Attire' takes the crown for branching, with as many as sixteen flowers per stalk. A clump is a bouquet. 'Black Comedy' is a dark purple with a striking orange beard. It is easily fertile, despite being from SDB × TB breeding.

Marky Smith has quickly become the Queen of the IB class. Her plan is a simple but effective one: cross the best SDBs (often her own or Paul Black's) with the best TBs (often her own or Keith Keppel's), and—no surprise—you get really nice

IBs. Marky also has the distinction of winning the first American Dykes Medal for an IB—her dark plicata 'Starwoman'. 'Starwoman' is a fine grower and has a beautifully branched stalk and lovely flowers, showing the influence of the wide SDB 'Chubby Cheeks' in its wide falls. The wild luminata-variegata 'Delirium' is appropriately named with its lemon-gold standards and falls boldly splashed with lavender purple, set off with orange-red beards. It also won a Sass Medal. A perfect companion to 'Delirium' is the bright-yellow 'Soleil', from a cross of a bright-yellow TB and an orange SDB. It has bright color and perfect form and is a vigorous plant. There are many yellow irises, but 'Soleil' is special. My favorites of Marky's newer IBs are those with exceptional bold colors. Combining her wild SDB plicata 'Droid' with Keith Keppel's 'Tuscan Summer', a vivid brown on yellow plicata, gave the amazingly bright-brown-on-gold plicata 'Salted Caramel'. Combining pink plicata TBs and SDBs gave rise to my favorite IB at present, the wildly marked 'Lakota', which has a strong-orange ground color and a violet luminata wash in the center of the falls and standards. The bright-orange styles, hafts, and fall edges just light up the flower. From an inspired cross of the black SDB 'Dark Matter' and the bold variegata TB 'Reckless Abandon' came the gold/black variegata 'Stormbird' and the gold/dark-red 'Mutineer'. Thank you, Marky, for giving us such a wonderful group of IBs!

Fascinated by the tet MTB and IB hybrids the Craigs produced, Philip Remaire set out to cross between these and TBs from the Keppel

ABOVE 'Salted Caramel' is an IB plicata of striking colors.

TOP 'Lakota' is one of the most striking and bright IBs produced to date.

BOTTOM The bright variegata 'Stormbird'

line. Both projects were successful. 'Love's Moment' is a beautifully branched pastel amoena with better form than many of the *aphylla*-derived IBs. It has proven to be an interesting parent for me. 'Violet Moon' is a clear and ruffled violet blue that reblooms heavily here in Oregon and is nearly MTB in size. 'Dalriada' combines the bright-orange tet MTB 'Sun Spirit' with the equally bold-orange TB 'Shivaree'. The result is a bold-orange flower in perfect IB size, and with lots of buds and branches. As you might imagine, this is a great landscape plant.

Old Favorites

'Frosted Cups' and 'Dilly Dilly' (Warburton). These are a wonderful pair of white and blue IBs with impeccable form and great growth. There were big clumps of these two in my parents' Massachusetts garden, and they never failed to put on a great display.

'Annikins' (Warburton). Of the early hybrids of TB × *aphylla*, this is one of the best. It has a glossiness to the navy-blue/purple color that was unique, and the form is exceptional for this type of cross.

'Bottled Sunshine' (Nichols). What a great flower! The 'Joyce Terry' pattern in TBs is one with strong-yellow standards and white falls bordered yellow. 'Bottled Sunshine' is a spectacular example of this pattern in the IBs, and a strong plant too.

'Dark Waters' (Aitken). When I gardened in Mississippi, IBs were sometimes unhappy campers, but 'Dark Waters' performed beautifully. In a climate where leaf spot was rampant, the foliage was always flawless.

'Rare Edition' and 'Vamp' (Gatty). These two IBs from Joe Gatty greatly popularized IBs. Both are amazing performers and grow well across the country. 'Rare Edition' is a crisp dark-violet-blue plicata, and 'Vamp' is an outrageous blend of red purples. Despite their age, they still look as though they belong in a garden populated with newer hybrids.

New Favorites

'Black Comedy' (Black). Although this is not the darkest IB I grow, it is dark and has a glowing orange beard that sets off the flower. Lots of buds and branches too!

'Dalriada' is an outstanding bright-orange color.

'Love's Moment' is a pastel amoena.

'Dalriada' (Remaire). Philip was working with Vicki Craig's tet MTBs and IBs, and this cross to the Keppel orange TBs gave the brilliantly colored and perfectly proportioned creation. This is one of the most refined of the *aphylla*-derived IBs.

'Fried Green Tomatoes' (Stout). What a great name. Standards are cream white, while the falls are a good, not muddy, gold shade of green—rare in the bigger medians.

'Hand Sewn' (Walker). This one was a bit of a surprise when I bought it at a local iris auction. Lee Walker has hybridized some nice Japanese and spuria irises, as well as a few MDBs. This IB is a respectable, clean-white IB with a neat stitched edge that reminds one of sewing.

'Lakota' (Smith). My favorite IB at present, 'Lakota' combines an unusually bright-apricot-orange ground color with a violet, center-of-the-petals luminata pattern on both standards and falls. This confined pattern makes the ground color really pop! An exemplary grower as well. It is fertile too!

'Line Drive' (Sutton). This is such a neat flower. Although plicatas are common, this flower is not; bold stripes on the falls take this flower to a new level.

'Love's Moment' (Remaire). This is a pastel amoena of lovely form and wonderful growth. What makes this plant a favorite is the branching and bud count, producing a cloud of these lovely pastel flowers. I would like a whole garden of plants like this.

'Salted Caramel' (Smith). A different flower with a strong-yellow base color and brilliant chestnut plicata markings. Like all of Marky's IBs, this has great plant habits and perfect flower form.

'Stormbird' (Smith). What contrast! Standards are a bright gold, and falls are near black. Perky form and a great stalk. A clump of this iris is a garden statement.

REFERENCES

Gatty, J. "Intermediates." *The Medianite* 26 (1985): 22.

Warburton, B. "Nature's Own Hybrid Intermediates." *The Medianite* 25 (1984): 62.

Miniature Tall Bearded Irises

Although MTBs are in the same height range as the IBs and the BBs, they have a distinctly different look because the flowers are no bigger than 6 inches (height + width) and the stems are pencil thin. Clumps tend to be dense because of their short rhizomes, resulting in little bouquets of dainty blooms. Their floriferous nature and graceful stalks make them flower-arranging favorites. Indeed, their first name, "table irises," suggested their usefulness in table arrangements (Peckham 1929; Witt 1978). The small flowers and short, flexuous stalks of the MTBs worked much better

A clump of the MTB 'Candy Basket'

than their taller relatives in arrangements. The current term, miniature tall bearded, was coined by Lee Lenz and approved by aficionados as one that better described the myriad uses for this group of irises, not limiting them to arrangements.

Like the BB class, the MTB class was initially formed by small selections—but from the diploid TB irises, not the tetraploids. These old diploid TBs that gave rise to the MTBs were staples of gardens in the 1920s and 1930s, chiefly hardy hybrids derived from crosses between *I. variegata*, *I. pallida*, and perhaps *I. cengialtii*. Small segregates of these crosses were produced by several breeders, but the first real attention they received was in the seedling patches of E. B. Williamson in Indiana. His daughter, Mary, and yearly garden visitor Ethel Peckham were enchanted by a number of "runts" that occurred in the seedling patch, and pulled these selections for a further look. They christened them table irises, which was probably a good marketing ploy. From these first selections, the all-white 'Pewee', lemon-yellow 'Siskin', pale-violet 'Bunting', cream with orange beard 'Daystar', and golden-yellow 'Kinglet' were introduced. Further crosses by Mary Williamson resulted in the clean-blue plicata 'Widget' and the pastel variegata 'Nambe'. Interest in the class had all but faded when, in 1952, Alice White of Hemet, California, ran an advertisement inviting people interested in table irises to join a round robin—a correspondence group—to study and save this group of irises. Luckily, the response was good and the group started to collect all the Williamson cultivars, plus other small irises from other breeders that might fit the class. Mary Williamson had defined the class under rather strict criteria so that members would know exactly whether an iris qualified for an MTB.

Here are the criteria that were circulated in every round robin:

- They bloom with the tall bearded iris.
- They range from 15 to 25 inches tall; best at about 21 inches.

One of the first Williamson MTBs, the white with bright-orange beard 'Daystar'

Jean Witt used the striped species iris *I. variegata* var. *reginae* to produce a series of striped and smooth MTBs.

- Flower is 2.5 inches tall × 3.5 inches across (or width + height = 6 inches).
- The whole plant, flower included, is small, perfectly proportioned.
- Foliage is narrow, graceful in proportion to the plant.
- Stems are wiry, graceful, slender, ⅛ inch to 3/16 inch under the bloom, ¼ inch under the last branch, and ⅜ inch to ⅝ inch at the ground line.
- MTBs are completely hardy in the northern states.

These guidelines allowed members of the robins to screen other varieties that might meet the class, and also determine if the seedlings they raised were true MTBs.

From these round robin members, a few other MTBs were ferreted out, including the delightful orchid 'Two for Tea', tiny plicata 'Pixie', Bliss's dark-violet 'Tom Tit', and Ricker's pale-blue 'Blue Mouse'. A series of mutants from the variegata 'San Souci' (Witt 1971) include the old gold 'Sherwin Wright'; speckled and splashed 'Kaleidescope' and yellow-splashed 'Joseph's Coat Katkamier' also fit the restrictive MTB standards. These additions gave a broader palette of color from which to hybridize. In the beginning, the going was rough. Intercrossing the MTBs produced seedlings similar to existing cultivars, and the fertility level was low. Seedling crops of fewer than twenty were typical, limiting advancement. A better approach was to cross small diploid BBs with existing MTBs because the color palette of the BB diploids was much greater, covering virtually all the colors in the diploid TBs. Some of the MTBs, such as 'Pixie', were termed "headshrinkers" in that when crossed to larger flowers they still gave MTB-sized progeny. Thanks to some incredibly dedicated workers, forms and colors began to improve, as did the fertility.

If you can flash forward seventy years from this tiny beginning, we have a class of iris of tremendous variety, with colors from white to dark purple and all sorts of interesting patterns, many not seen in any other iris group. Luckily, in the push toward more diversity in blossom colors, and forms, we haven't forgotten that wonderful, indestructible plant, and present-day MTBs are just as hardy as the ones selected from the Williamson patch in the 1930s. What is quite remarkable is the fertility of today's MTBs compared to their ancestors. I routinely grow over a thousand MTB seedlings from just a backyard (albeit a BIG backyard), and the bees set hundreds of pods on the blossoms that I haven't used in crossing. Since the early days, breeders have experimented with routes to MTBs other than the traditional diploid approach. Tetraploid MTBs, first envisioned and produced by Ben Hager, have allowed for the production of MTBs in the colors of the tetraploid TBs and BBs, chiefly adding pinks and dominant amoenas to the diploid MTBs color palette.

Garden Uses and Culture

Unlike many other irises, bearded or otherwise, MTBs can be used much like any other perennial in the border because they withstand tough conditions. In the mixed perennial border, clumps of MTBs planted near the foreground provide a focal point when blooming but also provide a mass of swordlike foliage throughout the season. Cultivars with purple-based foliage, of which there are many, provide even more interest. Because MTBs can be left undivided for more years than many irises, the clumps will get quite large before they require digging and resetting. Now, I'm not encouraging abuse—annually fertilizing near the clumps will keep things looking good. When I was growing up in Massachusetts, virtually every old garden had clumps of 'San Souci' (although we called it 'Honorabile' back then). Although they were never tended or fertilized, they bloomed beautifully every year. What more could you ask for a perennial? Luckily, we don't have to rely on 'San Souci' anymore; there are hundreds of cultivars in every color. Because most of the MTBs are fully dormant, they shed almost all of their leaves in the fall, making for easy cleanup and no chance of winter damage to the foliage. Ours survived minus 32 degrees Fahrenheit in Massachusetts, so there were no worries about winter losses either.

One of the most extreme uses for MTBs was in a Massachusetts garden that had steep banks. Nothing much would grow because the plants would wash away after heavy rains. The gardener cleaned the bank, put in a few rocks (ubiquitous in New England) to hold the slope, and planted MTBs between the rocks. Within a couple years the bank became a solid mass of MTBs, and what was once a bit of an eyesore became a focal point of the garden. I can't think of another iris that could hold a bank so well.

A narrow bed near my front walkway is planted solidly with MTBs, and it is one of my favorites. TBs would be out of proportion in that narrow space. Planting early and late varieties of MTBs, plus tucking a few MDBs along the edges, gives me a good six to seven weeks of bloom, and, because of its location, it's something I can enjoy every day during bloom season. Lynda Miller did a clever display of MTBs at a recent American Iris Society convention, making an undulating ribbon bed with MTBs planted along its entire length and backed by conifers and taller perennials. The scheme had great charm and set off the MTBs beautifully.

Although I occasionally use MTBs in beds to edge TBs, I generally don't like this effect, because the daintier blooms of the MTBs are often lost among the huge blooms on the TBs. Mixed in a bed with other medians and dwarfs, however, it works. The BBs offer all the same colors as the TBs but won't overshadow the MTBs. If you plant the whole series of medians and dwarfs, you'll have a couple of months of color and flowers for cutting. Win win!!

As mentioned before, MTBs were once called table irises because of their use in table arrangements. Indeed, the flexuous stalks of MTBs add an air of grace and floral interest to virtually any arrangement. MTBs are perfect for those who enter iris shows, because their clumps of bloom often provide several stalks of "Queen of the Show" quality. Even a poor exhibitor like me has won best in section with an MTB stalk.

Kinds of Crosses That Generate MTBs

Probably the best approach for generating MTBs is to cross existing diploid MTBs with each other. Although this type of cross gave mostly duplicates of existing cultivars when the original MTBs were intercrossed, the genetic background of today's diploid MTBs is much more diverse. My seedling patch has an amazing variety of colors and patterns—most of them from simple diploid crossing. Likewise, Mary Louise Dunderman's breeding program was essentially this sort of crossing, and she made major breakthroughs in form, color, and pattern.

As mentioned, a major breakthrough came from crossing diploid BBs and TBs with the existing MTBs, especially when "headshrinkers" such as 'Pixie', 'Pewee', 'Quail', and 'Spring Sprite' were used in these sorts of crosses. Jean Witt's pastel amoena 'Ice Fairy' is a perfect example of crossing the small

One of the original Williamson MTBs, the bright-yellow 'Warbler'

MTB 'Pewee' and the BB amoena 'Mrs. Andrist'. Many current hybridizers are still exploring this material found in the old diploids, using the distinctive 'Romeo' or other material saved by our friends in the Historic Iris Preservation Society to create new looks. My 'Elfin Artistry' is an example of recent use of this older diploid material, thanks to Phil Edinger's sharing of an unnamed diploid nicknamed "Mullinax Butterfly," a variegata-plicata from Fred Mullinax's collection.

A number of diploid species have played a role in MTB development. Jean Witt used the neglecta selection of *I. variegata* var. *reginae* in a number of crosses. Surprising Jean, it brought stripes to the progeny—bold stripes! These lines proved to be profitable for her, not only in striped progeny but in bold variegatas, blues, and plicatas. Bee Warburton, though, was the person who brought more species crosses into the MTB stew. Her early crosses involved *I. attica* onto tetraploid TBs, with the hope of bringing those pink color genes into the diploids. Although no pink diploids resulted, the hybrid 'Gabi' came from these crosses and contains genes from Daystar × *I. cengialtii* seedling, a small white flower with an orange beard that Bee said "would set seed on a doorknob!" I grew this plant, and she was right! Perhaps Bee's greatest contribution to the MTB cause was introducing *I. astrachanica* into the MTB gene pool. Bee received seed of this species collected at Kalmikji from Georgi Ivanovich Rodiondenko, and raised four virtually identical violet bitone seedlings. Although they differed somewhat from the prevailing view of this species (now synonymous with the dwarf species *I. scariosa*), Bee recognized their potential right away. They looked like tiny MTBs with many buds and branches. Bee named one but distributed all four of these. The clone designated as #1 turned out to be the best breeder. Bee crossed the clone she registered as 'Kalmikji', named for the collection site. A cross of 'Kalmikji' to the seedling from Daystar × *I. cengialtii* gave the dark neglecta 'Tyke'. Others were quick to use the astrachanica seedlings in crosses. Chief among these is 'Astra Girl', a tiny white that has been a boon in producing in-class MTBs.

Most MTBs are still diploids, but tetraploids from crossing small BBs with *I. aphylla* forms gave breeders seedlings that fit the MTB class. Dismayed with the fertility of the existing diploid MTBs, Ben Hager was one of the first to take this approach. His cultivars served as a basis for the breeding efforts of virtually every worker in the class. Although many of the early tetraploid MTB cultivars were too large in flower and too thick in the lower stalks, breeders have taken up the challenge. Many present-day tetraploids approach the size of the diploids. Ken Fisher, Jim and Vicki Craig, Thomas Johnson, Paul Black, and Lynda Miller all have produced MTBs from this approach.

A final approach is to cross diploids with tetraploid MTBs and small BBs. Although such approaches might give sterile progeny, surprisingly many of these are quite fertile. Dorothy Guild used small BBs, IBs, and SDBs in her crosses with MTB (Guild 1985). For some reason, when an *I. aphylla* derivative is involved in the cross, there is at least some fertility regardless of the other parent. As one might expect, some of the irises from such crosses don't fit exactly in any class of iris but have characteristics of several. Some of these will fit the MTB class, but others may prove to be useful breeders. In my own work, fertile IBs have been useful in crosses to tetraploid MTBs, as have taller, branched SDBs crossed with tetraploid MTBs. Some of these meet the strict MTB requirements, whereas others serve as breeding stock for the next generation.

History of Miniature Tall Bearded Irises

The first MTBs were small selections from the diploid TB lines. The first intensive effort on these irises occurred in the Williamson seedling patch in Indiana. E. B. Williamson was a unorthodox hybridizer. Instead of making planned (and recorded) crosses, he hired schoolgirls to pollinate whole fields of irises with mixed pollen. This shotgun approach did ensure that seeds from some combination of the parents would result, but gave no idea as to the identity of the parents. In these huge seedling patches, Ethel Peckham and E. B.'s daughter, Mary Williamson, began pulling the "runts," as E. B. referred to them, from the patches for further evaluation. Here is the tale of their origins, as Mary related:

> The Table Iris originated with us at the suggestion of Ethel Anson Peckham of New York State. She used to visit us each year at flowering time to check seedlings. As Ethel, Father, and I walked up and down the seedling rows, we were intrigued with several "runts" which appeared among the tall bearded irises and bloomed with them. We separated the runts from the rest of the irises for further study. We were completely charmed by the perfect balance throughout the whole plant. It was Mrs. Peckham who created the name "table iris," because of their usefulness in making table arrangements. Tall Bearded irises are much too large for such use. In our enthusiasm we set up standards for ourselves in selecting this type of iris.

A good selection of these runts was introduced, including the white 'Pewee', pale-violet 'Bunting', white with orange beard 'Daystar', golden-yellow 'Kinglet', lemon-yellow 'Siskin', and light-yellow 'Warbler'.

At one time, 'Pewee' was the most ubiquitous of the MTBs, used to border iris beds. It was the first winner of the Williamson-White Award.

These irises remained popular and were grown by many. 'Pewee' won the first Williamson-White Award in 1968, thirty-four years after being introduced. After her father's death, Mary attempted more crosses and introduced the important parents 'Widget', a blue plicata, and the pastel variegata 'Nambe'. Because of the Williamsons' use of mixed pollen to produce their seed, details of the parents behind the MTBs are scant at best. Mary did give some clues as to the possible parents of the MTBs:

"Most of the varieties used in breeding were such old favorites as 'Juniata', 'Shekinah', 'Archeveque' . . . "

The varieties she mentioned are older diploids, mostly from *I. variegata* and *I. pallida* crosses. On the basis of the foliage habit, size of the bloom stalk, and strong winter dormancy of the MTBs, it is more likely that they are predominantly of *I. variegata* blood. Additionally, variegatas are one of the most common patterns seen in these irises, further establishing their important role as the predominant force in producing the MTB class.

Charles Gersdorff was a scientist with the USDA and a registrar of the American Iris Society. Unlike the Williamsons, Charles used known parents to raise his MTBs. 'Shekinah' occurred frequently in his crosses, substantiating Mary's belief that this iris was behind the Williamson MTBs as well. In addition to 'Shekinah', Gersdorff used other small diploids and selections of *I. cengialtii* in his crosses. Charles called his plants "bedding irises," a most appropriate name since their use extended beyond table decorations. He registered around thirty in a fairly broad gamut of colors and patterns. Faced with criticism from iris judges and a general lack of interest in the smaller irises when hybridizers were trying to create larger flowers, Charles dumped all of these irises in disgust. That was a sad day for the MTB class, especially considering the limited color range in the existing MTBs of the day. One can only think of the progress that could have been made, had these irises not been destroyed. Luckily, interest in smaller irises, and MTBs in particular, was about to rebound.

Alice White of Hemet, California, had been quietly working with the MTBs and had introduced the plicata 'Angelita' and the variegata 'Smarty Pants' in the late 1940s. She ran an ad for people interested in table irises to join a correspondence group, called "round robins." Twelve people responded, and they and other robins that were subsequently organized started the process of finding other irises that might fit the class and start breeding for improvements. Alice continued to breed them and produced the pastel variegata 'Quien Sabe' (Spanish for "who knows," since the parentage was unknown), the bright variegata 'Smarty Pants', and the apricot-flushed lavender 'Buenita'. 'Buenita' was exceptional in regularly having twelve or more buds to the stalk. It is in the background of many present-day MTBs. In reading through Alice's notebooks, it was clear how difficult this breeding was: few crosses took, the number of seeds in each cross was low, and germination was erratic. Most years you could count on fingers and toes the number of seedlings. You had to believe that this was somehow going to pan out in those relatively dark days of the class.

Jean Witt was one of the original twelve people who joined Alice's robin in 1952, and she continued crossing until 2015. In that time period she won two Williamson-White Awards and numerous honorable mentions for her MTBs. The American Iris Society awarded her the Hybridizer's Medal in 2012 for her sustained and successful career. Her first introduction is the lovely 'Ice Fairy', a pastel-lavender-blue amoena from 'Pewee' × 'Mrs. Andrist'. It brought a notable enhancement in form to the class, with noticeably wider petals. 'Ice Fairy' went on to win the Williamson-White Award in 1973. Jean maintained several lines in breeding, but many stem from a cross of 'Blue Mouse' × *I. variegata* ssp. *reginae*. She nicknamed a seedling from this cross "Ecru Etchings" (a strongly lined blend). Bee seed from this parent went two ways in her breeding, with the blues 'Eowyn' and 'Sally Lightfoot' following the blue side, and 'Fair Haldis' and 'Shady Sands' from the more blend side of the family. (Jean once told me, "When your cross didn't take, plant the bee seed because you might not have anything to plant

Alice White's 'Smarty Pants' is a bright-lined variegata.

The introduction of Jean Witt's 'Ice Fairy' represented a startling advancement in form and helped popularize the MTBs.

otherwise.") The blues showed little of the old grainy blue typical of MTBs of that era but, rather, had color that was smoothly applied. After introducing Mildred Brizendine's 'Dancing Gold', Jean planted bee seed of this plant and selected out the deeper-colored and better-formed 'Spanish Coins'. This iris is a rapid grower, making pretty clumps, and garnered Jean her second Williamson-White Award in 1981. A bee pod on 'Spanish Coins' produced the brown-on-gold plicata 'Bronze Sprite'. Jean was concerned with form in the MTBs and liked those MTBs that had a gentle "fall flip," a gentle ruffle but not fussy tight ruffling that she considered too much. Her 'Jazzy Décor' was one of the first to have this, and although the pollen patent was unknown, she assumed it was 'Real Jazzy' because she made that cross but the tag had disintegrated. A bee pod on 'Jazzy Décor' gave the startlingly veined amoena 'Little White Tiger', with an even more accentuated ruffling to the falls. In looking through Jean's notebooks, it's obvious she thought long and hard about her lines for reds. If you look at the pedigree of 'Redrock Princess', Jean's ultimate red, you begin to understand her thought process. She thought the reds needed a specific sort of yellow to make the overlying red-purple color seem redder, and her reds had a mix of yellows behind them. I inherited much of Jean's breeding stock, and there is one truly red seedling among them, but it's a bit tall for a proper MTB. I hope my crosses with it will give one in-class with that same wonderful color. Jean had also been using the unusual diploid plicata 'Rhages', which had fine dots concentrated in the middle of the flower. Her 'Just a Dusting', which I selected from one of her final groups of seedlings, has this pattern, but with better form and a perfectly in-class MTB flower. It is a nice finish to a wonderful career.

Earl Roberts was, of course, most famous for his work in bringing pink SDBs into reality, but he also did a number of crosses for MTBs, and several of his first award winners were in this class. His first two, 'Parakeet' and 'Desert Quail', came from a cross of 'Widget' × a Welch seedling. 'Parakeet' is a pastel variegata blend with the colors of a wild parakeet, and 'Desert Quail' is a yellow-ground plicata with brown stitching. 'Mockingbird', a red-purple plicata, came from a cross of two old diploids—the strongly striped

This red seedling of Jean Witt's is one of the reddest bearded irises the author has seen, but the stalk is a little too thick for a good MTB.

'Just a Dusting' represents Jean Witt's efforts to produce an MTB, with the center dotting of its TB grandparent 'Rhages' in an acceptable MTB flower.

rose blend 'Navajo' and the French-lined plicata 'Demi- Deuil', bringing new cultivars into the MTB gene pool. It would win Earl a Williamson-White Award in 1970. Earl also added species into the MTB gene pool by crossing *I. variegata* ssp. *reginae*, *I. timofejewii*, and *I. pallida* into the MTB lines. 'Cedar Waxwing', a variegata blend in the tradition of 'Parakeet' but brighter and bolder, and 'White Canary', a pastel minimal plicata, are derived from some of these species crosses. Earl's series of bird-named MTBs would be the base of other breeders' programs. They were consistently in-class and had better form than their predecessors.

Although Walter Welch is the father of the movement to revive interest in dwarf irises, he also did substantial work with the MTBs. The origin of his irises is a little obscured, but this statement from a round robin letter gives a few clues:

> One of the most exciting progenies came from some bee pods on a seedling from *I. variegata* × Table which I had saved because it had yellow standards and falls near white though not full white. From this row of about twenty plants I named 'Topsy Turvy', 'Brown Crown', and 'First Time'. Imagine a range from white, yellow, brown bitone, reverse Pinnacle, plicatas, all in this small progeny. Apparently the Tables are heterozygous for several different patterns.

'Topsy Turvy', with strong-yellow standards and white falls, and the rich-brown bitone 'Brown Crown' have proven to be excellent parents for MTBs. Both had better form than the Williamson MTBs and produced interesting seedlings in a broad range of colors. Pastel and light 'Pale Amoena' has a similar nebulous pedigree, but what it lacked in pedigree, it made up for as a parent, breeding clean colors and good forms. 'Pale Amoena' gave the clear-blue 'Jill Welch' and the nicely formed variegata 'Ornate Pageant', plus, in the next generation, the contrasted variegata 'Welch's Reward'. 'Consummation' is considered Walter's finest MTB, and for many years it was untouchable in the amoena class. It has clean white standards and dark-purple falls rimmed white. It won the Williamson-White Award in 1985. Walter's MTBs proved to be marvelous parents for other breeders, and many other breeders' lines derive from these fine hybrids.

Dorothy Guild went after the fertility issue early in her hybridizing career. She found that the Sasses' 'Eversweet' and Williamson's 'Nambe' were easy parents, in contrast to most MTBs of that era, allowing her to raise larger seedling populations. As any plant breeder knows, it's a numbers game: the more progeny you see, the better your chances are to produce good progeny. From the 'Eversweet' × self cross, the seedlings segregated into both blues and striped seedlings that reflected the colors and patterns in 'Eversweet'. Dorothy selected the striped selections 'Tiger Doings' and 'Tiger Territory', the well-formed solid variegata 'Li'l Kitty Hawk', and the blue selection 'Elegant Try'. Here is an account of this 'Eversweet' progeny in her words:

> I don't particularly like the 'Eversweet' form; however, some interesting things came in that form, plus at least five other flower forms, and about twenty color combinations ranging from an off-white through yellow, red, brown, and many combinations of blue, violet, and purple. Some are selfs, but most are bicolors or have standards of one color, while the falls have cream ground with blue or red stripes, some heavy, some hairline.

Dorothy had one intriguing seedling from this cross, 63E9, which has brown standards and blue falls. Unfortunately, this plant was not introduced, although I have a seedling in that color range and I hope to honor Dorothy by naming it for her.

The best breeder of these early selections, from a 'Nambe' bee pod, is her 'Whispering Sprite', which was registered as a white with blue influence but is actually a pale plicata. It had better form than previous introductions and is an easy pod and pollen parent. One of my favorites of her early selections is the strong yellow with little metallic flashes that she named 'Glint o' Bronze', a seedling from Earl Roberts's 'Desert Quail' × self. 'Bit o'

Afton', from Warbler × self, is an orchid amoena with lots of buds and is near the height limit for the class, as is its parent, 'Warbler'. 'Bit o' Afton' has abundant pollen and is an easy pod and pollen parent; it garnered Dorothy her first Williamson-White Award in 1975. My favorite of Dorothy's straight diploid MTBs is 'Maggie Me Darlin', a brown blend that involves many crosses of Welch's 'Brown Crown' and some of Dorothy's diploids. A BB seedling of Victor Runberg's named 'Victory Pink' struck Dorothy's fancy—it was small flowered and had stems that were not overly thick for a tetraploid. It had a tangerine beard, something Dorothy would have loved to get into the diploid MTB lines. Amazingly, pollen from 'Victory Pink' set seeds on diploid MTBs, and diploid MTB pollen set seeds on it—normally such crosses failed or would set only a seed or two. One of the first seedlings from this sort of cross was the bright, tawny-rose blend 'Disco Jewel'. 'Disco Jewel' had the loud orange beard from its parent; it would win Dorothy her second Williamson-White Award in 1983. Dorothy worked diligently to try to get tangerine pinks in the diploid MTBs by crossing 'Victory Pink', 'Pagoda', and other small pink BBs and IBs into the diploid MTB lines. The two most promising ones in these programs were the rose 'Candy Lane' and the dusty orchid rose 'Dusty Ruffles'. These may be the closest to pink we will see in diploids. Dorothy should be congratulated for her spearheading the crosses of tetraploids into the diploid lines. These are difficult types of crosses to make and often have low germination rates, but Dorothy made steady progress. Her hybrids are in the background of many other workers, and the American Iris Society was well aware of these contributions, honoring her with the Hybridizer's Medal.

Mary Louise Dunderman almost single-handedly brought the MTB class to its current state. In her career, she made over 50,000 crosses and raised 20,000 seedlings. Now *that* is a major effort, especially considering the lower fertility and poor seed germination of the first MTBs. Keith Keppel was able to produce charts of her breeding lines (many are not fully detailed in her registrations), and from these charts you can see the generations of work it took to reach each of her goals. Her selections were made judiciously: virtually all of her cultivars were awarded an honorable mention, and five won Williamson-White Awards. In addition to these honors, the American Iris Society awarded her the Hybridizer's Medal in 1994.

Some of her pivotal early successes involved 'Widget' crossed with the orchid pinks BB 'Pink Ruffles' and MTB 'Two for Tea'. By combining and recombining these initial crosses, Mary Louise was able to create a series of orchid pink plicatas that hadn't existed in this class, starting with the classic 'Carolyn Rose' and continuing through 'Bettina', 'Rosemary's Dream', and—one of her last—'Crafted'. Each displays a different intensity and degree of marking. 'Carolyn Rose' has proven to be an exceptional parent. Besides the orchid-pink plicatas, more-typical blue plicatas also were produced from these lines: the minimally marked 'Tinsel' and the more strongly marked 'Doll Ribbons' are two outstanding cultivars.

'Maggie Me Darlin' is one of the few Dorothy Gild MTBs still in commerce and represents a combination of her best brown and blend diploid MTBs.

The Dunderman blue lines represent an offshoot of her orchid plicata lines; the blue plicata 'Widget' often produced blue seedlings of good color and form when crossed with self-colored irises. Mary Louise's blues include the light blues 'Blue Bisque', 'Blue Twinkle', 'Gingham Blue', and 'Surprise Blue', as well as the dark blues 'Todd' and 'Panda', the latter with a striking white beard in contrast to the petal color. It is amazing that such a variety of colors and patterns could descend from such a simple series of base crosses, but it shows the ability of a careful hybridizer to pull out these interesting characteristics.

The Dunderman white and yellow lines also derive from those initial crosses involving 'Widget'. The first of these is the pure white with frilly style arms named 'Clare Louise'. Unlike the Williamson white MTB 'Pewee', 'Clare Louise' had great fertility, both as a pod and pollen parent. In a cross to 'Pewee' it gave the much-improved 'Jana White'. This cultivar is used throughout the Dunderman lines because it gave its seedlings superior flower form, wider falls, and domed standards. A bee pod on 'Jana White' gave rise to 'Opal Imp', a white with falls that are sometimes flushed with blue. Further breeding from that line gave rise to the lovely formed 'Baby Bibs', a clean white with falls shaped like a baby's bib. The most outstanding advance in form from these lines is the crystalline-white 'Crystal Ruffles', which has minimal plicata markings but a tighter form and light ruffling. 'Crystal Ruffles' is an odd iris in that it has an extra chromosome, compared to the typical twenty-four-chromosome diploid MTBs, and has proven to be a frustratingly difficult parent. Indeed, the only seedlings I know from this iris involve crosses to tetraploid MTB—Stephanie Markham's white 'Mystic Crystal' and Paul Black's pastel plicata 'Lavender Sprinkles'. 'Mystic Crystal' has its parents' reduced fertility, but 'Lavender Sprinkles' is fertile. 'Chickee' is a cross of her white and yellow lines and represents a significant improvement in form and strong color. It has been a boon to getting good form into the MTBs.

The Dunderman red line was no less an effort. These lines combined the best of the old diploid reds such as 'Monarda' with small, bright-yellow segregates from her other lines to create irises with a strong-red color. 'Bellboy', a red bitone, 'Persian Lantern', a strong red violet with orange beard, and the cherry-red 'Cheese and Wine' were the only irises released from these lines. 'Cheese and Wine' has proven to be a useful breeder for many others, and it represents a culmination of these lines.

Thank you, Mary Louise, for producing all these wonderful flowers and raising the bar on the kinds of colors and forms we can expect in the MTBs.

Alta Brown, one of the early workers in the dwarf and median classes, added a lot of high-quality varieties, many with better form. Her first introduction, 'Dainty Dancer', is a pastel variegata like an improved version of 'Nambe' and became the basis for her other introductions. A cross of 'Dainty Dancer' × 'Blue Mouse' gave a great series: blue-violet bitone 'Dainty Bluebell', pastel amoena 'Dainty Dove', and pale plicata 'Dainty Cloud'. My favorite of Alta's MTBs is the brightly colored 'Quirk', a variegata, but the falls are white-veined wine red, with the veins coalescing in a spot at the end of the falls. 'Quirk' proved to be a useful breeder for many colors and patterns.

Ben Hager was an early proponent of the MTB class but quickly felt that the diploid path was too difficult for achieving better forms and colors. In fact, he believed that the diploid approach would produce only cultivars that were essentially like first- or second-generation crosses of *I. pallida* and *I. variegata*. Instead, he sought a route through the tetraploids. Although he was unable to grow *I. aphylla* clones in his California garden, Wilma Greenlee sent him pollen of 'Thisbe' and other clones so that he could use these to cross to small BBs. Even in the first generation, Ben was able to select seedlings that had the requisite flower size and stems that fit the class, except perhaps for the lowest parts of the stem. These tetraploid MTBs tended to bloom before the diploid MTBs. From this first group of seedlings Ben introduced dark-purple 'Shrinking Violet', amber-yellows 'Scale Model' and 'En Route', both from the BB 'Robert Melrose' × 'Thisbe', and 'Entract', from the pink TB 'June Bride' × 'Thisbe'. Ben crossed these first-generation seedlings to small BBs and sib, and intercrossed them to produce a family of tet MTBs.

Virtually all of the subsequent tet MTBs can be traced back to the Hager lines. 'New Idea', the second-generation introduction, represented a significant improvement in form and is an interesting sort of rosy purple with an orange beard. 'Puppy Love' is from a combination of 'New Idea' and several different pinks. Iris breeders call their bad seedlings "dogs," and I think by naming this one a "puppy," Ben was acknowledging that it was not a perfect flower. It had ungainly form, but pink it was. However, in the next generation, a cross of the well-formed yellow 'Louise Hopper' and 'Puppy Love' gave the much-better-formed 'Abridged Version', as well as the "Little trio"—'Little Me', 'Little Who', and 'Little You'. All have better form than 'Puppy Love' and offer clean lemon-yellow, peach, and blended colors. Other hybridizers have successfully used these MTBs in crosses. Ben's most impressive achievement, formwise, was 'New Wave'. It was a revolution in form, having a classic TB shape reduced in all proportions. Although not a fast grower, it was useful in hybridizing to bring more modern form to the class. Besides these MTBs, Ben left us a few other tet MTBs in other colors: brick-red 'Gumdrop', pastel-blue-violet 'Tit Willow', pastel blend 'Style Model', and yellow-splashed 'Ingenious Paradox'. Thank you, Ben, for creating an essentially a new class of iris! If you study Ben's pedigrees, you see that this did not happen overnight. Many generations of seedlings were raised, and only his hybridizer's sense that he was on the right path kept him going.

Riley Probst is the king of variegatas! His line actually goes back to a seedling of Ann Probst, his late wife, from 'Quirk' × 'Amethyst Sunset', called 'Pretty Quirky'. This iris turned out to be a useful parent, and a cross to 'Real Jazzy' gave the bright and contrasted 'Pretty Jazzy'. A cross of 'Pretty Quirky' with 'Welch's Reward' gave one of my favorite irises, 'Plum Quirky', a more pastel variegata with lemon standards and lavender-washed falls. 'Plum Quirky' has good form and passes it on to its children. For me, it blooms a bit later than most MTBs, extending the season. 'Holiday in Mexico' is the newest of these variegatas, with falls veined in violet and a nice form. Both 'Plum Quirky' and 'Holiday in Mexico' won the Williamson-White Medal.

Jim and Vicki Craig were challenged by famed TB and median breeder Gordon Plough to use *I. aphylla* in crossing to produce smaller versions of the TBs. This was no easy task, although they were aided by Ben Hager, who shared similarly derived seedlings. Bee Warburton's *aphylla*-derived IB 'Maroon Caper' and several different clones of *aphylla* were also used in their lines. If you look at the pedigrees

'Plum Quirky' is one of Riley Probst's variegata MTBs and has outstanding form and clean colors.

of the Craig MTBs, you can see that Rome was not built in a day. Not all of these early ones were consistently in-class in certain areas of the country, but four of their last ones seem to be close to diploid MTBs in character, and these have proven to be fine parents as well. 'Night Spirit' is a well-formed dark purple with a self beard and gentle ruffles. 'Spell' is a pastel amoena pattern with lovely form and copious branching. 'Maidenhood' is a white with near-tangerine beards. My favorite of these is 'Sun Spirit', a bright orange (a first in the MTBs) that goes back to the Hager TB oranges and a bewildering array of crosses with the *aphylla* derivatives. The Craigs should be congratulated for their dedicated work on a difficult project.

Ken Fisher started his hybridizing in Minnesota but moved to a rocky plot of land in Bella Vee, Arkansas, for most of his career. Ken bred both diploids and tetraploids and did much work crossing tetraploids into diploids to try to achieve the colors and patterns of tetraploids with the more petite proportions of the diploids. Sometimes these hybrids have reduced fertility, but others appear to be stable diploids or tetraploids. Some also appear to be misclassified as tetraploids, because many breed as good diploids.

Regardless of their ploidy, these are some fine irises. Of the early and surely diploid irises, 'Frosted Velvet', a seedling of Welch's outstanding 'Consummation', rates highly and kept its status as best amoena for many years. 'Chocolate Fountain' is one of my favorites of the Fisher irises and has deep-brown standards and falls solidly a good blue purple. Although listed as from a tetraploid cross, it has the small anthers typical of diploids and crosses easily with them.

The irises discussed below are all listed as having some mixed heredity, although again, they breed easily with diploids and have characteristics of diploid MTBs. 'Steffie' is a wonderful spotted amoena with an almost typical SDB spot of blue on white falls. 'Blue Harmony', 'Stitched in Blue', and 'Garden Standout' are great and well-formed plicatas. These have various extents of a stitched plicata pattern and are well formed and vigorous. An unusual plicata is the splashed red-violet-on-cream 'Autumn Splash', which has a distribution of color I've not seen on any plicata. Blues in the diploid MTBs are difficult, but 'Sailor's Dream' and 'At Last My Blue' are both well formed and have less of the grainy look of many older blue MTBs. 'Look Here' is a nice variegata with cleaner hafts and more red-toned falls than most. Some of the Fisher irises do appear to be tetraploids, all of them tangerine factored or dominant amoena. 'Fashionable One' in orchid bitone with tangerine beards, 'Pink All Over' in clear salmon pink, clear-yellow 'Marjorie L', and interesting lined variegata 'Delightful Dulaney' are good examples that seem to stay well in-class.

Jack Norrick introduced only four irises, all of them MTBs. Two were pivotal for the popularity of MTBs. 'Bumblebee Deelite', a brilliant variegata with beelike colors, was revolutionary for its tight clumps and was popular at several AIS conventions. The clumps look like a sea of little bees. It was the first MTB that made a good showing in voting for the Dykes Medal. 'Lucky Mistake' is out of the smooth-blue Welch MTB 'Jill Welch' and is a better-formed and more lavender-blue version of its mom. It turned out to be a fantastic parent, passing its smooth coloration and fine form to its progeny.

Clarence Mahan was a student of iris history and published *Classic Irises and the Men and Women Who Created Them* (2007), which chronicles the development of iris hybridizing from its beginnings. He also did some hybridizing, chiefly with the MTBs. His 'Reminiscence' is a fine neglecta that went on to win the Williamson-White Medal. One of the few good, clear whites is 'Robin Goodfellow', and it makes fine clumps. My favorite of Clarence's MTBs is the appropriately named 'Petit Louvois', a brown bitone that resembles the classic Cayeux TB 'Louvois'. 'Petit Louvois' is from a wild cross of the dark bitone 'Black Lady' and Dunderman's orchid-pink plicata 'Carolyn Rose'. With that pedigree, it has proven to be a interesting parent.

Lucy and John Burton are median enthusiasts who were influenced by the many other Median Iris Society members in Massachusetts. Their first success and Williamson-White Medal winner is 'Billie the Brownie', pastel tan with peacock flash of blue. Their 'Isabella Anna' is a bright variegata derived from Jean Witt's bright yellow 'Dancing Gold'. 'Spring Muslin' is a vigorous plicata with the branching habit of its pollen parent 'Astra Girl'. 'Ginger Treat' was popular at several American Iris Society conventions and is an approach to red with a strong infusion of yellow. It's from yellow × red breeding, much as to what Jean Witt prescribed for pursuing reds.

A protégé of Mary Louise Dunderman, Terry Varner used many of his mentor's plants but also used species, older diploids, many of the Welch cultivars, and some tetraploids in his breeding work. His first crosses were directed toward producing darker MTBs, since the flowers of many were more pastel. Both 'Valiant Warrior' and 'Velvet Bouquet' are nice dark neglectas, with a bit of velvet on the falls. Dark flowers are not the only area Terry tackled, since he made a significant advance in blue MTBs with his 'Deserving Attention', a clear and quite true blue. Terry was one of the first to use *I. astrachanica* in crossing, and his tiny white with gold beards 'Astra Girl' is an outstanding plant, floriferous and well branched and an interesting parent. Even in crosses with much-larger flowers, it gave MTB-sized flowers. His 'Astra Lady' is a bit bigger and broader white flower from 'Baby Bibs' × 'Astra Girl'. Terry was not a fan of plicatas and threw many away before selecting his marvelous 'Manisses', a nicely formed amoena plicata, and the yellow-ground plicata

TOP 'At Last My Blue' represents Ken Fisher's best approach to diploid blues.

BOTTOM 'Autumn Splash' is an unusually marked plicata.

ABOVE 'Delightful Dulaney' is a probable tetraploid with a unique fall stripe.

'Tracking'. One of my favorites of Terry's is the improved 'Consummation' he named 'Among Friends', a well-formed and well-contrasted amoena. Despite MANY tries, I have yet to set a pod on this cultivar, unfortunately. Due to a family illness, Terry had to discontinue his hybridizing program, but luckily he shared three outstanding seedlings with Stephanie Markham that she registered for him. 'Sun Charm' is to me the best of the diploid yellows so far on the market, with lovely form and great color retention. It is also an outstanding parent. 'Adazzle' is a nice lavender with a bright-orange beard. It has some tetraploid genes in it too, so that beard might be tangerine. 'Cherry Wine' is one of the darkest-red MTBs. It makes a tight clump and is a floriferous plant. Thank you Stephanie for saving these three outstanding MTBs.

Lynda Miller is a fellow Oregon transplant, leaving behind Indiana's dicey iris-growing climate. 'Bangles' was her first big success in the MTBs. With its amethyst standards, bluer falls, and fine shape, it went on to win both the Franklin Cook Cup and President's Cup for the best iris at two conventions, the only iris to do so. It was an easy winner of the Williamson-White Medal. To follow that theme, Lynda introduced the popular contrasted variegata 'Baubles and Beads', which also garnered a Williamson-White Medal. Lynda has a sense of humor with names that winked at Indiana's inhospitable climate. The pastel variegatas 'Survivor' and 'Dodger' were the only seedlings that survived a hailstorm. Those are tough iris! Since arriving in Oregon, Lynda has continued the diploid lines. Outstanding among the new irises is 'Moose Tracks', with strong lines, red-brown standards, and nearly black-lined falls. It is on track to win another Williamson-White Medal. Lynda's new 'Off the Grid' is a 'Moose Tracks' kid, but this time in a variable plicata in the same tones as 'Moose Tracks'. 'Zipped Up' is a boldly marked navy-on-white plicata. Two of my favorite new variegatas from Lynda are 'Canby Gem' and the neatly marked 'Emoji'.

In addition to diploid MTBs, Lynda has been working with tetraploid MTBs "that look

TOP 'Deserving Attention' is one of the bluest of the diploid MTBs.

MIDDLE Derived from her popular 'Moose Tracks', Lynda Miller's 'Off the Grid' is a wild brown on gold plicata with irregular splashes.

BOTTOM Vividly marked plicata 'Zipped Up' has a pattern of stripes, lines, and dots that make for a bright and intriguing flower.

like diploid MTBs." I think she is coming close to this goal. Starting with husband Roger's 'Ben a Factor' (which combines Craig and Hager lines), Lynda has cranked out a series of winners. 'She's a Doll', in pink standards over lavender falls, comes close to "the diploid MTB look." The flowers are small and the stalk is thin and well branched. It is turning into a great parent for tet MTBs. The line has also produced the bright-coral-pink 'Coral Sunrise', pastel variegata 'Rose City', raspberry-pink 'Raspberry Shocker', and the even-deeper raspberry-to-red 'Probie'. These tets add the full palette of tangerine tones to the MTBs that are not found in the diploid gene pool. Lynda's latest tetraploid introductions include the yellow-and-blue bicolor 'School Colors' and the rust-colored 'Dweeb', the latter a new color in the tetraploids.

Barbara and David Schmeider have hybridized two of my favorite MTBs: 'Peebee and Jay' and 'Pixel Packin' Mama'. (These get kudos for the best names too!) 'Peebee and Jay' looks much like what you'd expect: peanut butter–colored standards and grape jelly–colored falls. This is one bright iris and won the Williamson-White Medal. 'Pixel Packin' Mama' is from the reciprocal cross that generated 'Peebee and Jay' but is quite different. The standards are a more subdued blend of brown and violet, and the falls are cream with dots of purple virtually covering the falls. Both Schmeider irises are vigorous and are proving to be fascinating parents.

'School Colors' is a clean tetraploid MTB with yellow standards and blue falls.

I have known Stephanie Markham since we were "the kids" growing up in Massachusetts and surrounded by the greats of the median and dwarf world. Stephanie fell in love with MTBs after seeing a large planting at Ken and Aggie Waite's garden in western Massachusetts. Her early work started with some of the now-classic hybrids of Terry Varner, Ken Fisher, and Mary Louise Dunderman. Her first two success stories were the incredibly vigorous blue-violet plicata 'Larry's Girl' and the smooth-orchid-pink 'Dancing Lilacs'. Some of my favorites are Stephanie's series of plicatas, many heavily dotted, including blue-violet 'Speckled Spring', red-violet 'Going Dotty', and strong variegata plicata (and occasional erratic type markings) 'Syncopated Rhythm'. Stephanie used Varner's streaked novelty type 'Cyber Net' in many of her crosses, and this has generated some interesting progeny in the clean and bright variegata 'Fernie Bridge'. The next generation produced the lovely 'Pixie Painting', white with irregular blue splashes. Her series of amoenas are all outstanding, including the orchid-pink-striped 'Razzleberry Dressing', bold violet amoena 'Jiggity Jig', and my favorite, the smooth 'Bit o' Royalty'. Stephanie's most famous introduction is her Williamson-White Medal winner 'Hot News', a brick to rose-red blend with a bright-orange/tan beard with excellent form. It is derived from the Dunderman reds and a yellow seedling of Terry Varner's, echoing Jean's idea that a good yellow base is needed to give a good red flower. Stephanie is also pursuing crosses with many of the older diploids with unique colors and patterns. She produced some exciting progeny, such as 'Pluie d'Or', 'Romeo', and 'Minnesota Mixed Up Kid', by using *I. astrachanica* derivatives to shrink the flowers and stems to proper MTB size. There should be lots more exciting things coming from Stephanie's seedling patch in the near future.

Chuck Bunnell was greatly influenced by the hybridizing work of the Norricks. The Norrick iris 'Lucky Mistake' has turned out to be an exceptional parent for him. It is behind two of his best irises, 'Hoosier Belle' and Dykes Medal–winning 'Dividing Line', a first for MTBs. Both these irises are neglectas but are quite different: 'Dividing Line' has a distinctive light line down the middle of the falls, whereas 'Hoosier Belle' is a more classic neglecta but with exceptional form and branching. Alice White's 'Buenita' was a distinctive color break in an apricot variegata. Chuck's 'Breakfast in Bed' is a great improvement over that classic, with beautiful color and form. My only frustration with this iris is its limited fertility. Chuck's second Williamson-White Medal winner is the maculosa 'Gesundheit', with a bright-yellow ground color and irregular speckles of vivid purple. Chuck introduced four outstanding plicatas, each quite different. 'Lite Sprite' is a pastel and irregularly marked blue-violet plicata. 'In My Veins' and 'Nick of Time' are yellow-ground plicatas with strong lines and stitches of purple. My current favorite of the Bunnell plicatas is 'Pixi -Wan Kenobi', a cream ground with strong lines and stitches of tan rose. It has lovely form and a perfect stalk. Chuck's new 'Heavenly Dream' is the first MTB that combines a yellow ground with the orchid-pink plicata markings, and it has wide petals for a diploid. Although Chuck has introduced only a few MTBs, he has created some of the most popular and beautiful

ABOVE Stephanie Markham's Williamson-White Medal winner 'Hot News' is bright red with wonderful growth habits.

TOP Delicate 'Pixie Painting' is white with irregular markings of violet.

BOTTOM 'Razzleberry Dressing' recalls a fanciful dessert from *Mister Magoo's Christmas Carol.*

MTBs on the market. Certainly, winning the Dykes Medal for an MTB was no easy trick!

Paul Black has produced a number of diploid and tetraploid MTBs of merit. In the diploid lines, the plicatas 'Huggable You' and the splashed 'Scrambled' are outstandingly vigorous. 'Scrambled' has the broken color added to the patterning. 'Lilac Wings' is one of the rare orchid colors in the diploids and has a strong-orange beard. 'Juvenile Joy' is my pick of the Black diploids, an unusual mix of brown-veined standards and red-black-veined falls. It's a interesting parent too. Paul's

TOP A clump of Dykes Medal winner 'Dividing Line'

BOTTOM LEFT A single flower of 'Dividing Line' showing the distinctive pale line down the middle of the falls, reflective of its name

BOTTOM RIGHT The appropriately named 'Gesundheit' with strong-yellow flowers heavily splashed with purple

first tetraploid introduction, 'Blue Chip Stock', came from an inspired cross of the tetraploid MTB 'Echo Pond' and the SDB 'Privileged Character' and is a neat blue neglecta. Paul's 'Flirtin' Skirts', a rose purple with bright-apricot hafts and styles, is a similar unusual mix of IB, small TB, and SDB in the pedigree. Despite this wild pedigree, it is amazingly fertile. 'Queen Mum' has a similarly mixed pedigree and introduces a bit more ruffling than the typical MTB. I podded my plant of 'Queen Mum' heavily because I thought it was such an important break in clean colors and form. We haven't seen a good new tet yellow in a while, but Paul's 'Bright Victory' is that plant. Paul has introduced a number of MTBs from a variety of approaches, and I look forward to blooming them and using them in crosses in my garden.

TOP 'Heavenly Dream' has pastel yellow ground color with orchid-pink plicata markings, the first of its type.

BOTTOM 'Bright Victory' is the best of the recent yellow tetraploid MTBs.

TOP 'Queen Mum' represents a real leap in form in the tetraploid MTB and also a clean pink color.

BOTTOM 'Booyah' is one of the strongest MTB variegatas, derived from the classic MTB 'Bumblebee Deelite'.

As a teenager I corresponded with Dorothy Guild and Jean Witt. Both of them supplied plants that would be useful in my program. In a year when no hand-crosses took on the MTBs, I took Jean's advice to "plant the bee seed." Three hundred seedlings resulted from these seeds, and Bee Warburton declared it "the biggest patch of MTBs ever." From these bee pods, three MTBs were introduced. 'Little Bluebeard', from a 'Widget' bee pod, was the first blue-bearded blue MTB on the market, and a good clean flower. 'Real Jazzy' was for many years the brightest of all the variegatas, with chrome-yellow standards and red-violet falls with a neat edging of the same chrome yellow as the standards. It inherited its good form from its parent, 'Topsy Turvy'. 'Real Jazzy' has turned out to be a wonderful parent. The third MTB, this one from a pod on 'Whispering Sprite', gave the spritely pastel plicata 'Tammy's Tutu'. After a nearly forty-year hiatus, I was able to start breeding MTBs again. 'Purple Petite' is a bright purple with red-violet hafts and a strong-orange beard from a cross of 'Cheese and Wine' and 'Cherry Berry'. It is a floriferous and vigorous plant. A cross of Guild's 'Maggie Me Darlin' and the Schmeiders' 'Peebee and Jay' gave the full-brown 'Peanut Butter Cup', with tiny flowers on well-branched stalks. 'Booyah' is a bright and smooth variegata from a cross of the ever-popular 'Bumblebee Deelite' and Stephanie Markham's clean, contrasted amoena, 'Bit o' Royalty'. 'Booyah' is a much-wider flower, and the falls have almost no haft markings, a nice improvement on the classic 'Bumblebee Deelite'. 'Elfin Artistry', a yellow-ground plicata, is derived from an unnamed variegata plicata from Fred Mullinax's collection. These antique diploids add a lot of genetic diversity to the relatively narrow

'Elfin Artistry' is a tiny flower with a pattern of both yellow and purple dots, lines, and spots.

TOP 'Peanut Butter Cup' is a bright-brown MTB with marvelous branching.

BOTTOM 'And Stripes Forever' displays the strong veining (stripes) as well as the fall flip that Jean Witt championed.

base in the diploid MTBs. 'Ring Around the Collar' recalls the old Whisk commercial with a distinctive brown band around the amber standards. 'And Stripes Forever' is one of a series of striped MTBs coming from the author's work. It is on the short side for MTBs, at about 18 inches tall, and making clumps more like an SDB.

Most of the efforts in hybridizing MTBs have been in the US, but Olga Wells in the UK developed a number of MTBs that were highly regarded and won awards from the British Iris Society. Even her Dykes Medal TB is really a tall IB! I thank her for sending comments on these plants as I was writing this chapter. Some of these outstanding irises have made their way to the US as well. 'Medway Valley' is a dark variegata-type blend with brownish standards and falls strongly marked and shaded purple. A cross of 'In Fashion' to 'Medway Valley' produced the neat red-violet-on-cream plicata 'Staplehurst'. 'Bockingford' is a pale plicata out of Terry Varner's 'Creme Lady'; a cross of it with the classic 'Bumblebee Deelite' gave the bright and well-formed variegata 'Headcorn'. 'Teasaucer Hill' is a well-formed yellow with white patch on the falls. Olga's 'Thruppence' is a most unusual plicata in cream with pale-brown markings and is derived from an SDB × IB cross. Her seeds that I purchased from the BIS seed exchange produced two good pink MTBs, which supports the idea that 'Bees Knees' was involved in the pedigree. These seedlings cross easily with the *aphylla*-derived tetraploid MTBs.

Old Favorites

'Ice Fairy' (Witt). This is one of the first irises that I purchased as a new introduction in 1966, and it still grows in my garden some fifty years later. It was the first MTB with significantly wider parts. It is a pastel amoena with the falls lined in pastel lavender blue. It is a frustrating parent like its mom 'Pewee', with little functional pollen, and the pods that it makes are often small.

'Buenita' (White). This was one of Alice White's that I loved as a kid. It had more buds than you can imagine, sometimes eighteen on a stalk. No other MTB has come close. The color was interesting, too, apricot with a lavender blaze on the falls, and what most would call tangerine beards.

'Real Jazzy' (Vaughn). Bee Warburton visited my garden the day this seedling bloomed. She wrote me a note saying that she "couldn't think of anything else on the way home. Your brilliant variegata is amazing." It has chrome-yellow standards and bright-red/violet falls neatly edged in chrome yellow. It was also the first MTB to have

'Real Jazzy' was an iris from the author's childhood seedling patch that still finds favor.

'Rayos Adentro' is Spanish for "rays within." It has prominent veins that extend from the hafts, contrasting greatly with the white ground color.

the "fall flip" that Jean Witt so admired, and it became a breeder for that form. It is on the shorter side of the MTB class, making a striking low clump.

'Crystal Ruffles' (Dunderman). One of the most well-formed diploids ever introduced in a sparkling white (although plicata marks are buried deep in the flower). This, together with Dunderman's 'Chickee', set the standard for form in MTBs. Unfortunately, 'Crystal Ruffles' is an aneuploid and makes few normal gametes; the few seedlings are from crosses with tetraploids.

'Maggie Me Darlin' (Guild). This is one of Dorothy's last introductions, and one of her best. It combines a lot of the approaches to brown in one flower in a two-tone effect of brown, with purple expressed on the falls. Despite having what could be drab colors, it is not at all dull. It has given me some nice seedlings.

New Favorites

This is a hard list for me because there are many I like. We are lucky to have so many pretty ones. I have purposely not listed my hybrids in this section, although some are favorites.

'Breakfast in Bed' (Bunnell) and **'Tyrone' (Zuraw).** These two irises are my "modern Buenitas" because they are apricot gold, and 'Breakfast in Bed' is actually a descendent of 'Buenita'. Both have a nice shape and are such different shades of this color you will want both in your garden. Neither are easy parents, but I have had better luck with 'Tyrone'.

'Deserving Attention' (Varner). This blue MTB received little attention from the judges, but in a class derived primarily from gold and red *I. variegata*, getting a good clear blue is no mean trick. This is that blue. Form and growth on this one are really good; it may be my favorite of Terry Varner's introductions.

'Rayos Adentro' (Morgan). What an exciting flower! Standards are dark red / purple, and falls are cream, heavily veined the same or darker red purple. Form, branching, and plant habit are great. It is proving to be a champion parent as well.

'Black Cherry Sorbet' (Harris). Chad Harris is a renowned breeder of Japanese irises, but he fiddled with some MTB crosses involving 'Redrock Princess' and came up with this brighter red, aptly described by its name. Nice form, and fertile.

'Moose Tracks' (Miller). I saw this plant before it was introduced, and went berserk! It is such a wild thing. Lots of stripes of dark red / brown on a cream base fairly shout at you. For me it grows on the short side for MTBs, about 18 inches, and makes pretty low clumps.

'Hot News' (Markham). Producing garden-worthy red MTBs has proven to be a challenge for hybridizers. 'Hot News' is close to that goal. It is much redder than its predecessors and has nice form. The colors are blended rose and browner reds, and it is a maniac plant too. If it would set seed more readily, I would be a happier camper!

'Just a Dusting' (Witt). When I inherited Jean Witt's seedlings, there was not much information in her stud book about this plant, although a brief description and pedigree were there, so it was quite a surprise when it bloomed for the first

'Black Cherry Sorbet' has beautiful form and a colorful pattern of red veins on a cream background.

time. 'Just a Dusting' is a nicely formed, cream-white flower with violet dots in the center of the falls. Although it has no pollen, it sets seed easily.

'Pixi- wan Kenobi' (Bunnell). Such a cool flower. The standards are rose purple dotted with cream, and the falls are lined with white and sport the same rose-purple dots as the standards. Really nice shape and great growth habits make this one a winner.

'Chocolate Fountain' (Fisher). When I first saw this flower at the 2015 regional convention, I was bowled over by its vivid colors of chocolate-brown standards and blue-purple falls.

And a couple tetraploids:

I really prefer diploid to tetraploid MTBS, but I'm gradually warming up to some that have more of the diploid look and that are reliably in-class. Two of the Craig MTBs make me happy, though, and many hybridizers have used them. I'm sure some of Lynda Miller's and Paul Black's new ones will make this list as they become more permanent inhabitants of my yard.

'Sun Spirit'. A nice, bright shade of apricot orange with good growth and form. It has lots of buds and dense stalks that rival the diploids.

'Spell'. This one is more subtle than 'Sun Spirit': white with a thin band of light blue around the falls (the "Emma Cook pattern"). It has an excellent stalk and one of the best-formed flowers of any tetraploid.

REFERENCES

Peckham, E. A. "Table Iris." *Bulletin of the American Iris Society* 31 (1929): 29–31.

Guild, D. "Pink MTB: Where Oh Where? Not Here!" *The Medianite* 26 (1985): 44.

Mahan, C. E. *Classic Irises and the Men and Women Who Created Them*. Malabar, FL: Krieger, 2007. 404 pp.

Witt, J. G. "Notes on Honorabile." *The Medianite* 12 (1971): 88–90.

Witt, J. G. "Miniature Tall Bearded Irises." In *World of Irises*. Edited by B. Warburton and M. Hamblen, 122–130. Wichita, KS: American Iris Society, 1978.

'Chocolate Fountain' is a vivid combination of chocolate-brown standards and blue-violet falls.

'Sun Spirit' is one of the last MTBs from the Craigs' long breeding program and is consistently in class.

6

Border Bearded Irises

The border bearded or BB class of irises was a "created class" formed from tall bearded-iris seedlings that were shorter than 28 inches but too cute to pitch. They have all the colors and patterns found in the tall bearded iris, plus some unique ones that have been brought into the BBs from dwarf irises. Harold Knowlton was one of their early proponents. In the 1950s and 1960s in Massachusetts, it was common practice to edge the beds of tall bearded irises with the species hybrid 'Paltec' or the white MTB 'Pewee'. Their small flowers and old-fashioned form made them inferior to the TBs behind them, but Harold Knowlton began saving the shorter seedlings, using them to edge the beds of tall bearded irises. He affectionately called them his "runts." Geddes Douglas came up with the more appropriate term "border bearded" (BB) irises for the group. These small selections were especially good at the corners of the beds, where a tall bearded would look way out of proportion for the site. Harold's 'Pearl Cup', 'Buttonhole', and 'Cricket' were perfect examples of the kind of irises he wanted. They were small versions of tall bearded, reduced in all proportions.

A clump of the BB 'Lady of the Night'

Because of Harold's promotion of these irises, the Knowlton Medal, awarded each year to the top BB iris, was named in his honor.

In the early days of the Median Iris Society, there was considerable discussion about the BBs' ideal flower size. Some favored larger flowers on shorter stems, which created a blob of color, while others favored the better-proportioned look. Fortunately, the latter view won out, and we now want flowers with a combined height and width of less than 8.5 inches (preferably smaller) and with stalks shorter than 28 inches, and foliage proportionately smaller as well. In these early years, hybridizers and growers measured flowers and stalks of BBs that were considered well proportioned along with those that weren't. These studies resulted in a formula for the ideal proportion: 3–3.5 inches × (height + flower diameter) = height of stalk (Wright 1967).

Many of the plants that came from straight tall bearded breeding with these smaller sizes were actually runts—stunted because the plant was weak. The release of these runty BBs gave the class a bad reputation at first, though their reputation was restored through efforts to breed vigorous BBs. Now a grower can pick out a BB with reasonable assurance that it will stay small and be a vigorous garden plant. Still, it is wise to shop for BBs described as "proportionate" or "small flowers" to ensure that the plant is a true BB rather than a runty TB.

BBs are my favorite class of iris because they have the charm of the smaller bearded iris, coupled with the sophistication of the tall bearded class. To me, that's the perfect combination.

Garden Uses and Culture

BBs are still at their best when planted on the edges and corners of beds of tall bearded iris. Almost all iris growers grow some of the popular tall bearded irises. I grow the tall bearded irises in 6–8-foot-wide rectangular beds with clumps interspersed in the center of the bed. The BBs form a solid edging, with a good clump on each of the four corners. Years ago, Irene and Don Tufts carried this effect further by planting BBs that mimicked the color and patterns of the tall bearded irises, creating a sort of a "mini-me" approach. So, a TB with a certain color pattern was planted in back of a BB with the same colors and patterns. It was a charming effect, although some of the BBs, such as the uniquely colored gray blend 'Jungle Shadows', had no counterpart in the tall bearded class.

Another way to use BBs is in beds of their own. Lynn Markham was the first person I know who did this. Her kidney-shaped beds featured clumps of BBs grown to perfection. My own garden contains some narrow beds in which tall bearded irises would look out of proportion, but BBs fill the bill nicely.

If you live in a windy region, BBs can be a more attractive alternative to tall bearded irises. When I lived in Mississippi, for example, it seemed that a strong wind and rainstorm would flatten the tall bearded irises just as they were coming into bloom. Not a good look! This also happened in 2019 here in Oregon, when two weeks of wind and rain knocked over virtually every TB stalk. With their shorter stalks and smaller flowers, the BBs never suffered that fate.

I segregate my BBs from most other perennials, but two perennials—penstemon and *Dianthus* spp. (pinks)—are perfect companions culturally and aesthetically. Like the BBs, they don't need summertime mulching or watering. The pinks' blooming period coincides with the BBs' bloom, and the penstemons will continue flowering through much of the summer months. (Companion plants are discussed in more detail in chapter 7.) With a large amount of cultivars in these two diverse genera, there are all sorts of colors and patterns from which to choose, and the bed will be colorful for months

Culturally, BBs are more like tall bearded irises than the other median classes. Although some of the newer BBs that have some dwarf iris species in their background increase at a rate comparable to the IBs, many of those from straight tall bearded breeding benefit from a bit more fertilizer and more frequent division than the IBs or MTBs require. My rule of thumb is to let the BBs clump for three or four years before dividing them. Any longer, and bloom quality begins to suffer. Vigorous cultivars will need to be dug and divided more often. Save the good rhizomes and bring in fresh soil before replanting, or move them to a new bed (see more on culture in chapter 7).

One group of BBs, in particular, is a reliable component of the perennial border: diploid BBs primarily descended from *I. variegata* or *I. pallida* (or both). These are rock hardy; they are completely deciduous and tolerate crowded conditions and more summer moisture than BBs from tetraploid lines. When I was a kid, they grew in virtually every garden, passed from gardener to gardener over the years. 'Pink Ruffles' was a stalwart. A more modern example is 'Network'. A white, strongly veined with dark purple, it is Jean Witt's diploid derived from *I. variegata* var. *reginae*.

Kinds of Crosses That Generate BBs

TB Dropouts. As mentioned previously, BBs were sort of a "found" class resulting from small selections of tall bearded crosses. This is still the primary way new BBs are created, although it is not the most productive route. Creating a perfectly proportioned miniature version by crossing two much-larger cultivars, as you might imagine, is almost like winning the lottery! Fortunately, there are many fine examples of lottery winners. A number of tall bearded parents carry genes for small size, and the pinks, reds, and blacks produce many small seedlings, although many do not qualify as a good BB. Two of the Dykes Medal winners from the 1960s, 'Whole Cloth' and 'Rippling Waters', regularly produced BB-sized seedlings of excellent proportion. Dykes Medal winner 'Brown Lasso' is a beautifully proportioned BB out of a tall bearded cross. Because so many tall bearded-iris seedlings are raised each year, new BBs can come from this sort of crossing. Many BBs that are fallouts from tall bearded crossing are prone to grow out of class in different climates, so more-productive approaches to producing BBs have been tried.

BBs on purpose. Since the 1960s, hybridizers have been deliberately making crosses for BBs, taking several approaches. Crosses of BB with other BBs and to smaller, well-proportioned tall bearded have netted many fine irises. Crosses between BBs often yield fewer seeds than crosses between tall bearded irises, but the seedlings from such crosses are mostly BBs and small tall bearded, so the breeder has more selections from which to choose. Using this line of breeding, Myrtle Wolff, MayBelle Wright, Carol Lankow, Terry Aitken, Bennett Jones, and Lynn Markham have given us a number of wonderful, well-proportioned BBs in a wide color range. Myrtle's approach was extreme. She threw away any seedling with big foliage before it bloomed, so that only BB seedlings would survive and bloom. MayBelle Wright became increasingly convinced that BBs around 22 inches tall would be ones that stay in class in all climates. She called these BBs "bantams"; her yellow-and-white reverse bicolor 'Miss Petite' was an outstanding example. Stalwart BBs such as 'Yellow Dresden', 'Miss Ruffles', 'Angel Feathers', 'Tulare', and 'Marmalade Skies' have been used to great effect as parents for BBs. 'Marmalade Skies' was an especially effective parent, yielding almost 100 percent BBs in crosses even with tall bearded irises. Terry Aitken combined small tangerine lines with 'Brown Lasso' and came up with a line of surefire BBs in a wide range of colors.

Dwarf species. Small bearded-iris species have been used to cross with the BBs or smaller tall bearded, giving rise to plants with consistently smaller stature as well as vigor and hardiness from the dwarf species. Bennett Jones used the *I. reichenbachii* derivative 'Progenitor' to produce a series of amoena and Emma Cook pattern BBs, culminating with the Knowlton Medal winner 'Crystal Bay'. Keith Keppel used 'Progenitor' in crosses with plicatas to produce a strain of bicolor plicatas, including the Knowlton Medal winners 'Mexicali', 'Picayune', and 'Shenanigan', that owe their small size to both 'Progenitor' and a BB-sized seedling from the Sass breeding program. These Keppel irises are behind a number of current BB breeding lines. Joe Ghio used *I. balkana* to create a series of small irises, many with a deeper blot of color just beneath the beards. These Ghio hybrids include the well-proportioned and vigorous 'Passport' and 'Copy Cat'. Combining the Ghio and Keppel lines, Burch's 'Miss Nellie' is a consistent and vigorous BB that has proven to be a useful parent. It is behind the Vaughn and Burton BB lines.

Although both *I. reichenbachii* and *I. balkana* were useful in breeding BB, *I. aphylla* has been an absolute boon to progress in BB breeding. Ben Hager was one of the early proponents of this approach, although much of his work centered on obtaining tetraploid MTBs. Jim and Vicki Craig were the first to pursue *I. aphylla* in a purposeful way, creating a number of tetraploid IBs, MTBs, and BBs from this approach. What *I. aphylla* contributes besides its small size is a beautiful branch habit with many buds and often a low branch near the stalk base. Although the early generations of these lines had less sophisticated flowers (*aphylla* often produces lax flowers), persistence by hybridizers has resulted in BBs that have the stamina, vigor, and branching of the *aphylla* parent but with the sophistication of the BBs derived from TB breeding. Lynn Markham's and Paul Black's lines that descend from that line of breeding are especially fine examples of vigorous BBs, with copious branching and exquisite flowers. Crosses of these flowers between them or to BBs from unrelated lines give a majority of BB-sized seedlings.

When I was young, the IBs were considered a waste of time to use in breeding because they were thought to be sterile or nearly so. However, several prominent breeders used them, even back then, to add extra recessive traits from the tall bearded to the SDBs; the alternate path, crossing IBs onto BBs, was not used much until recently. IBs are strong growers, and it was thought that infusing them into the BBs might give the BBs the vigor they needed. Carol Lankow had a line of seedlings she called her "46 chromosome hybrids" from crossing IBs (forty-four chromosomes) with BBs (forty-eight chromosomes). Her 'Friday Blues' is an outstanding example of this work. When Barry Blyth introduced the IB 'Zing Me', he reported that this cultivar was a fertile IB. In addition, 'Zing Me' carried the strong spot pattern on the falls from *Iris pumila*, a pattern not seen in the BBs. Barry introduced a whole series from 'Zing Me' crossed to TBs, and Ed Baumunk introduced the popular 'Zingerado', a white with a spot of greenish yellow that came from crossing 'Zing Me' with the TB 'Silverado'; hence its unusual name. Marky Smith did a full-scale study of this issue by crossing numerous IBs with TBs or BBs (Smith 2005) and found that many IBs were quite fertile and gave a preponderance of small irises. From these crosses, 'Immortal' and 'Pecoro' were introduced. Keith Keppel's apricot-and-cream 'Sorbet Swirl' is from similar breeding and is a reliable BB. In these sorts of crosses, the IB parent contributes a variable set of gametes, and as a consequence, there is quite a bit of segregation of traits, including 12-inch-tall stalks with TB-sized flowers, and tiny flowers on a 36-inch stalk.

History of BBs

Here we'll discuss the work of breeders who have actively pursued BBs. There were many who introduced a chance small seedling from TB breeding that proved to be a useful breeder for the class: Don Denny's 'Am I Blue' is a classic example. However, most of these efforts resulted in runts or poor growers, giving the BBs a black eye in the iris world. Early on, large flowers on short stalks were registered as BBs, and there were proponents of these color blob types. Now, however, a BB must be no more than 8.5 inches (height plus flower diameter), and only well-proportioned flowers are the rule. The following hybridizers gave the BB class the distinction it enjoys today.

As noted, Harold Knowlton was the first to appreciate the value of shorter irises. Several of the tetraploid TB lines, chiefly those dependent on a large amount of *I. variegata* inheritance, such as the yellow-ground plicatas and recessive amoenas, consistently gave BB-sized seedlings. Harold's 'Cricket' (a bright variegata), 'Pearl Cup' (a pastel amoena), and 'Buttonhole' (a yellow glaciata) were perfectly proportioned BBs and set a class standard. Harold had many others in his seedling patch when he passed away in 1969. He was a lawyer and obviously felt comfortable in a suit, tie, and hat, even during garden tours, and everyone addressed him as Mr. Knowlton. Although that was considered proper in those days, I can't think of a single person who dresses like that today!

In the early 1950s, everyone was breeding pink TBs, and the pink TBs often gave rise to smaller seedlings that were pulled from the patches. Margaret Albright introduced two just before the American Iris Society recognized BBs as a class. 'Yellow Dresden', a clean lemon yellow, and 'Yum Yum', an apricot pink, were vigorous in-class plants. Both proved to be useful parents, and they are behind many of the BB lines of others. 'Yellow Dresden' won the first Knowlton Award in 1959.

Bennett Jones was exploring similar pink lines when he produced two BBs that grew in class and sparked interest. Salmon-pink 'Pagoda' and exotic-pink/dark-orchid-pink bicolor 'Frenchi' were consistently in-class and at the shorter end of the BB spectrum. Both plants would find their way into the breeding of not only BBs but tetraploid MTBs as well. 'Pagoda', especially, had small flowers and slim stems, useful qualities for breeding tet MTBs. Despite 'Frenchi' being introduced more than sixty years ago, it is still grown by a number of gardeners and offered for sale by the Historic Iris Preservation Society. 'Frenchi' won both the Knowlton Award and later the Knowlton Medal when the award was converted to a medal. Bennett did not stop with these two irises. Bennett combined the fertile IB 'Progenitor' with blue TBs, producing the blue amoena BB 'Glacier Bay' and the exciting Emma Cook–type 'Crystal Bay' in white with a blue band around the edge of the falls. Bennett was the first to exploit the smaller proportions of the IBs to produced well-proportioned BBs. 'Crystal Bay' garnered him a second Knowlton Medal. The coppery-brown 'Carnival Glass' was from straight breeding for browns, but these lines also relied heavily on *I. variegata* and similarly often threw short seedlings. 'Carnival Glass' was well proportioned but a slower grower than Bennett's other BB selections. His brilliant, almost metallic-blue 'Botany Bay' was a highlight of the 1968 American Iris Society convention in Stockton, California. 'Botany Bay' was obtained from a cross with the reliable light-blue BB 'Little Dude'. Bennett's 'Rain Pool' from 'Botany Bay' × sib has more of the pastel-blue coloring of 'Little Dude', and better form. Bennett was modest to a fault. When he authored the BB chapter for *The World of Irises* (Jones 1978), Bee Warburton and Melba Hamblen added positive comments about his BBs. I had the pleasure of meeting Bennett at several iris conventions. He was a kind and gentle man as well as an impressive hybridizer. His later work was chiefly in SDBs, and he revolutionized work in that area too.

Myrtle Wolff had a long and distinguished career, breeding plants mainly from her own line. She religiously pulled out and threw away the seedlings with too-big foliage. Now *that's* dedication to the cause! Myrtle's first two BBs were winners and perfectly in-class. She used the classic Schreiner black TB, 'Black Forest', which was registered as a TB but was really a good BB at 24 inches tall. A cross of 'Black Forest' to her TB 'Perfect Love' gave the two BB classics introduced in 1962: 'Debbie Ann' (in blue) and 'Timmie Too' (in dark violet). Both were vigorous growers and made cute clumps of bloom and went on to garner the Award of Merit. Myrtle's later introductions were in two groups, one descended primarily from her first two, and a tangerine line descended from the 'Yellow Dresden' and other tangerine-related BBs of the day. In the first group, the best irises included the pastel bicolor 'New Dew' and the dark purple 'Tanya Elizabeth'. Both were outstanding and could hold their own today. The yellow-tangerine line includes the bright-yellows 'Vallie Echo' and 'Teryn Leigh', orchid 'Senior Prom' (a name inspired by her granddaughter's prom gown), and pastel apricot 'Pampered Baby'. All of Myrtle's BBs were in-class, and most were vigorous growers.

Helen Reynolds was a true character of the iris world. Her catalogs featured clever quips, and she even drew insects that she had allegedly squashed in the margins! She lived to be a hundred years old and was active to the end. When the Sass brothers sold out, Helen introduced the wildly colored 'Jungle Shadows', an instant hit. 'Jungle Shadows' is an odd blend of gray, purple, and bronze, unlike anything on the market in any class. It quickly won the Knowlton Award and later the medal. Helen introduced two seedlings from it that are improvements in color and are even more in-class: 'Girl Guide' in an unusual gray blue, and 'Boy Scout', an olive and brown (close to the khaki of the Boy Scout uniform). Both won Awards of Merit, and 'Girl Guide' still grows in my garden.

It was actually Ben Hager who introduced 'Jungle Shadows' for Helen Reynolds. Ben was an early proponent of the BB class and gave them good coverage in his Melrose Garden catalog. Two of his most famous BBs—the pastel clear pink 'Pink Bubbles' and the deeper, salmon-pink 'Something Special'—were dropouts from his TB breeding, but he also made extensive use of his *I. aphylla* lines. The first of these, 'Star Child', was a first-generation species cross, but others, such as red-bearded white 'Audacious' and maroon 'Conjure', are from advanced generations. Oddly, Ben did not use many of his tet MTBs until later in his hybridizing career. However, the cross of his 'Pink Bubbles' with a seedling from that line gave him a bonanza of perfectly proportioned BB seedlings—the trio of orchid 'Brain Child', clear-pink 'Cupid Smiles', and pastel-apricot 'Brain Child'. As one might expect from that pedigree, all three were fine growers with in-class form and flowers.

Tell Muhlestein was heavily involved in pink TB breeding. He operated a commercial nursery that introduced irises for a group of hybridizers, chiefly those from Utah. These included the Albright BBs 'Yellow Dresden' and 'Yum Yum'. Tell made the cross of 'Golden Flash' × 'Yellow Dresden' and found that virtually all of the seedlings were in-class BBs. Tell introduced 'Lacy Lu' and 'Saucy Pink' from this cross and 'Tangerine Flash' from the F2 of this line. Bee Warburton repeated the same cross in quantity, and I was lucky enough to see that row of seedlings—hundreds of BBs in yellow, tan, orchid, pink, and apricot. Bee named only 'Lace Valentine', which went on to win the Knowlton Medal. However, another four or five could have been introduced from that cross. I still have memories of a bright yellow with a tangerine beard from that cross.

MayBelle Wright was a champion for the BB class. Although her first introduction, the ruffled blue 'Miss Ruffles', occurred as a dropout from TB breeding, the BBs became her focus. Most of her work involved 'Miss Ruffles' because it was reliably in-class and fertile. Crossed with Dykes Medal winner 'Rippling Waters', it gave her a bunch of wonderful BBs. 'Blue Treasure', a slight reverse amoena, was her pick of these. Her 'Miss Petite' (1972), a cross of 'Miss Ruffles' with 'Yellow Dresden', was what she described as a "bantam"-style border iris, on the lower end of the height range for BBs and guaranteed not to exceed the 28-inch height limit. Her pink BB 'Pink Kewpie' (1976) is a fine clear pink that grows well. Unfortunately, MayBelle left us too early, a victim of cancer. Many of her seedlings were further distributed by Glenn Hanson and Carol Lankow, and these have been used in breeding lines for both BBs and SDBs.

Alan Ensminger, the self-proclaimed "Wizard of Odds," didn't set out to make BBs. His goal was to make a blue plicata with a red-beard TB in his initial cross of the blue plicata 'Belle Meade' and the red-bearded white 'Frost and Flame'. In further crosses with these lines, and incorporating the BB maker 'Rippling Waters', he came up with a series of BBs in both self colors and with stripes and splashes of colors. It is a classic examples of "when life gives you lemons, you make lemonade." The most famous of these is the appropriately named 'Batik', a white broadly splashed with a dark blue / purple. It was a popular novelty and went on to win the Knowlton Medal. 'Calico Kid', 'Iris Bohnsak', and 'Varied' continued this splashed pattern into other colors and patterns. My favorites, though, are his self-colored BBs: the smooth, crushed-berry-purple 'Berry Rich', the bright-yellow 'Brighten the Corner', and the clean-pink 'Zink Pink'—a combination of Hager's 'Pink Bubbles' and his splashed BB lines. Another odd one is his 'Feathered Friend', a white with heavily laciniated petals that look like feathers!

A trip to Lynn Markham's garden to see the BBs and TBs was a must in the 1960s. Lynn's BB program was grounded in her cousin Marilyn Sheaff's breeding program, including the reliably in-class BB 'Little Lynn'. A cross of 'Little Lynn' to a white seedling gave the ruffled white 'Angel Feathers" After a hiatus of a few years as she put three children through college, she resurrected 'Angel Feathers' as a stud plant, and it quickly showed its ability to make a whole family of BBs. 'Teapot Tempest', a bright violet, is a direct cross of 'Angel Feathers' and the dark-purple TB 'Pops Concert'. It won the Knowlton Medal and is a good representative of the BB class because it makes excellent clumps. 'Secret Weapon', a slight reverse amoena, has a Warburton seedling with an interesting genetic stew of 'Progenitor', *I. aphylla*, blues, and yellow amoenas in the pedigree. 'Secret Weapon' proved to be a genetic powerhouse and is behind many of her subsequent introductions. 'Simmer' is a result of a cross between "the Feathers line" into the Stahly dark-purple BB lines and is a smoky reddish blend. With perfect proportions and potent pollen, 'Simmer' has proven to be an outstanding parent. Crossed to the odd TB blend 'Twilight Blaze', it produced the wildly brown-violet and red blend 'Dance Gypsy'. An outcross of the 'Simmer' line to Lynn's TB 'Other Voices' produced the unusual 'Devil's Waltz', which appears different each season in my garden: sometimes gun-metal gray, other times heavily flushed violet, and often with a metallic sheen—a fun flower. One of my current favorites is the pastel bicolor luminata 'Dapple Dawn'. The pedigree on this iris literally has everything but the kitchen sink in it, and it has proven to be an interesting parent because of this genetic mix. Lynn's hybridizing career shows that even a small patch of seedlings can add measurably to the field of median irises.

Carol Lankow was MayBelle Wright's protégé when she lived in Minnesota, and one of the few people allowed access to MayBelle's seedling patch after her passing. Carol rescued several plants that

TOP 'Simmer' is a beautiful velvety-red purple.

BOTTOM A clump of the BB 'Dance Gypsy'

were key to her subsequent breeding program. Carol's first BB introduction, 'Sounder', is a clear white with excellent proportion. A seedling of MayBelle's 'Ruffled Cherub', it inherits many of that plant's fine qualities. The dark-navy-blue 'Classic Navy' also derives from MayBelle's lines. It has a timeless quality and will always be in my garden. Carol crossed IBs with BBs to add an influx of vigor and reliability. 'Friday Blues' is a seedling of Carol's fine IB 'Friday Harbor' and Terry Aitken's TB 'Fly with Me'. The latter is a seedling of 'Memorable', a good breeder for BBs. 'Calico Cat' is what Maybelle would describe as a "bantam" BB, with stalks about 20 inches tall and well-proportioned flowers. Its pedigree involves both the IB 'Andi' and the reliable BB 'Miss Nellie', itself a product of an advanced generation of lines descended from *I. reichanbachii* and *I. balkana*. Thus, 'Calico Cat' incorporates the genes of three dwarf bearded species. It went on to win the Knowlton Medal. In the tangerine shades, her pink amoena 'Peach Ice Cream' and apricot-orange 'Mango Smoothy' are both in-class plants that are great growers. Carol, too, left us early, but luckily all of her seedlings were later introduced by Terry Aitken.

The BB 'Dapple Dawn', with a distinct luminata pattern and bright-lemon shoulders

Paul Black is in every chapter of this book! He has long been a champion of all the median and dwarf classes. Paul's BB work mainly involves incorporating the small size, candelabra branching, and vigorous habit from *I. aphylla*. These crosses were also the source of his small-flowered TB lines. The small-flowered TB 'Dolce' combines the Schreiners' white *aphylla*-bred IB 'Northern Jewel' and the Hager tetraploid pink MTB 'Abridged Version'. 'Dolce' proved to be a willing parent, giving rise to the nicely formed and vigorous (and well-named) 'Fleece as White' and the apricot/lemon 'Bundle of Love'. Both of these irises are Knowlton Medal winners and are reliable in a variety of climates. 'Bundle of Love' is an exceptional parent as well. I'm infatuated with three of the second-generation BBs from 'Bundle of Love'. 'Venus Blush' has copper standards and cream falls edged with copper, and a bright-orange-red beard. This plant has absolutely perfect proportion and makes one of the most lovely clumps of any BB I have grown. 'Grace and Charm' is a tiny BB with orchid standards and pinkish falls and a glowing tangerine beard. 'Fair Play' is a vigorous BB and great garden plant with light-yellow standards and lavender falls. 'Merry Mulberry' is a wonderful shade of rosy orchid with the most exceptional branching habit. 'Stylish Choice' is my pick of Paul's BB plicatas. It too has a dose of *aphylla* through his tet MTB 'Silver Ice', and lovely proportion and form. Crosses of 'Stylish Choice' to my 'Preppy' line gave uniformly nice and in-class BB plicatas.

Keith Keppel has produced some of the finest and most consistently in-class BBs of any hybridizer. Gifted with the IB 'Progenitor' from Paul Cook and intent on producing amoena plicatas and variegata plicatas, he made a cross to the TB plicata 'Royal Band'. Two generations later, out came the perfectly proportioned BB 'Mexicali', with gold standards and cream falls strongly marked dark red / purple. It was an easy Knowlton Medal winner and a good parent as well. The next generation produced the neat 'Picayune', a gold/white with strongly marked plicata hafts and a jaunty flare.

It has absolutely perfect proportion and won the Knowlton Medal in 1982.

Another Knowlton Medal winner was the cool amoena-plicata 'Petite Ballet', although this also goes back to the same original cross of 'Progenitor' and 'Royal Band'. Keith combined the amoena-plicata lines with the tangerine-bearded plicatas, resulting in the pastel-pink plicata 'Peccadillo', and in the next generation the wildly contrasted pink/purple 'Shenanigan'. Both of them won Knowlton Medals. 'Shenanigan' still lives in my garden, and its shocking colors still excite each spring. Later introductions featuring tangerine-factored plicatas include 'Rinky Dink' and 'Faux Pas', the latter a luminata. Keith has also experimented using IBs to cross with BBs and TBs. His blended creamy-apricot 'Sorbet Swirl' and cream 'Art Glass' are outstanding examples of this type of breeding. Keith has been lucky in finding BB fallouts from his TB lines, starting with the vigorous blue plicata 'Embroidery', which was the classic BB plicata for many years. His purple 'Snazzy' is extremely bright and vigorous; its extravagantly ruffled seedling 'Costume Jewelry' is more to the violet side. Keith has also produced a series of pink/violet bicolor BBs. Outstanding examples includes the boldly colored 'Wisecrack', apricot-and-violet 'Boondoggle', and the more subtly colored 'Adolescence'.

Others have found Keith's BBs to be wonderful parents. One of the most useful descendants from the Keppel lines was James Burch's 'Miss Nellie' from Ghio's balkana derivative 'Copy Cat' × 'Mexicali'. 'Miss Nellie' is a pastel variegata near amoena with darker-red-purple hafts, belying its plicata heritage, and with the deeper fall blot compliments of balkana. Unlike many BBs, 'Miss Nellie' is extremely vigorous and resistant to rot.

ABOVE The well-proportioned 'Bundle of Love'

TOP 'Merry Mulberry' has one of the best stalks of recent BBs.

BOTTOM Paul Black's 'Stylish Choice' comes from tet MTB lines and is reliably in class.

Lucy Burton used 'Miss Nellie' to produce the ultravigorous 'Margaret Beaufort', from a cross to the tetraploid MTB 'Louise Hopper'. Thus, 'Margaret Beaufort' has small-size genes from three species: *I. aphylla*, *I. balkana*, and *I. reichenbachii*. I crossed 'Miss Nellie' with the BB 'Stanza' to produce the bitone striped plicata 'Preppy' (2000). 'Preppy' is a vigorous grower and in the South is a wonderful rebloomer, sometimes right to Christmas. Crosses of 'Preppy' to other BBs or TBs give virtually all BB seedlings .The red plicata 'East Hampton' arose from a cross of the TB plicata 'Exactitude' and 'Preppy'; 'Foxy Doll' (also derived from Keppel BBs) × 'Preppy' produced the lumi-plic 'See My Etchings'. Keith, thank you for giving us this valuable genetic resource.

Hal Stahly produced several fine BBs that involve crosses between the black-and-orange TBs, which have traditionally been smaller flowers than other color groups. From straight black breeding came the velvety black 'Drum Solo', which won the Knowlton Medal. 'Fiddler' in red violet, 'Ignition' in darker violet, and brightly colored 'Combustion' are products of the black lines and orange lines combined. In addition to these BBs from his other lines, Hal also used the great BB 'Pink Bubbles' to produce the two nice pink BBs, 'Allie Sunshine' and 'Up Tempo'. The Stahly dark BBs have proven to be interesting parents and are behind many of the current crop of dark BBs.

Dave Niswonger must be the luckiest BB breeder ever! First, he rescued the seedling iris that became the first BB Dykes Medal winner, 'Brown Lasso', and later picked out a number of BBs from his TB breeding lines. Dave's first BB success was his beautiful 'Raspberry Sundae', a lovely shade of mulberry pink with red beards

TOP Keith Keppel's lovely glaciata BB 'Sorbet Swirl'

BOTTOM Outrageously colored 'Boomdoggle'

ABOVE Red-violet plicata BB 'East Hampton'

that also descends from BB breeder 'Rippling Waters'. 'Marmalade Skies', his charming BB with pink-standard/apricot falls, was derived from breeding pink amoenas, including the small-flowered TB 'Sunset Snows'. 'Marmalade Skies' turned out to be an excellent parent for BBs. One hybridizer proclaimed that "'Marmalade Skies' × anything gives 100 percent BBs." Well not quite, but I agree that it gave a majority BB seedlings.

Terry Aitken made an inspired cross of Dykes Medal winner 'Brown Lasso' and his orange BB 'Maid of Orange', hoping to combine the tangerine factors with the reverse amoena and banding patterns from 'Brown Lasso'. Several generations later, he produced the "Bonanza Cross", where all sorts of colors and patterns appeared in the progeny: reverse amoena 'Cut Above', yellow with tangerine beard 'Banana Royale', white with red beard 'Coconut Frosty', and orange 'Art Festival'. I still grow another sibling in the most unusual shape of orange overlaid with rose, and it is one of my favorite irises. The next generation from this line gave the neatly ruffled strong reverse amoena 'Buoyant Spirit', the peach 'Papaya', and 'Banded Rose' and 'Banded Gold', both with strongly banded falls. All these irises have nearly perfect proportions. Terry found that the blue TB 'Memorable' often produced well-proportioned BBs, and from such crosses came the lovely, ruffled blue 'Maui Surf' and the purple 'Maui Magic'. What is likely Terry's most widely grown BB is one of his first, the red bitone 'Cranapple'. Despite many attempts at crossing, nothing has resulted from this iris. A pity, too, because we need more red BBs.

Marky Smith is best known for her work with SDBs and IBs, but she has also produced a wonderful series of BBs that descend from her IB work. As mentioned previously, IBs were generally considered infertile, but Marky persisted in using them in crosses and produced a whole series of wonderful BBs that have fine proportions; many also have the vigor of IBs. These include the bright luminata 'Jaguar', the pastel glaciatas 'Immortal' and 'Truant', and the dark-violet with orange beard 'Benedictine'. Although these might show some fertility issues because of their presumed forty-six chromosomes, all have been fertile for me and seem to produce seedlings with especially good plant habit. My favorite is the peach blend 'Perquisite', which descended from Terry Aitken's 'Bonanza' line. 'Perquisite' is a nearly perfect flower with excellent proportion. The luminata 'Picaro'

'Banana Royale' was one of the seedlings from Terry Aitken's "Bonanza Cross" that gave BBs in a variety of colors and patterns.

'Cut Above' has the dark top from the 'Brown Lasso' side of the pedigree plus tangerine factors, making it an interesting blend.

has some of the finest proportions of any BB; even the foliage is slender and short. It is a high-quality iris, and one I hope to use in hybridizing.

Rick Tasco has several nice BBs that involve IBs or taller SDBs in the pedigree, so they are some of the most well-proportioned BBs of any breeder. 'Magic Quest' is a cool plicata with dotting in the center of the falls and a nice flaring form. 'Sheer Excitement' is a vigorous purple luminata that won Rick his first Knowlton Medal. 'Frosty Spirit' is a frosty light blue with deeper beard. Despite their mixed-chromosome pedigrees, they have proven to be fertile parents for me.

Although the BB class has had some rough going, we have benefited from breeders who purposefully breed for reliable BBs. Some of my favorites are listed below. These have all proven to be good growers and in-class plants, and some do well both in Mississippi and Oregon.

Old Favorites

'Brown Lasso' (Buckles-Niswonger). This is the first BB, (actually the first median iris) to win the prestigious American Dykes Medal ('Orinoco Flow' won the English Dykes Medal), and this honor is richly deserved. A prominent brown ring around the falls gives it great distinction. Nearly perfect proportions and good growth. Although 'Brown Lasso' is not an easy parent, it is behind the banded BB line of Terry Aitken and Calvin Helsley's BBs 'Sing Praises' and 'Carousel Waltz'.

'Girl Guide' (H. Reynolds). Helen Reynolds introduced the last of the great Sass brothers' breeding lines, including the uniquely colored 'Jungle Shadows', using it in crosses to produce 'Girl Guide'. The flower is an odd shade of gray blue with perfect BB proportions and vigorous growth. Although 'Jungle Shadows' is often marked with virus stripes, I have not seen this on 'Girl Guide'.

'Orinoco Flow' (Bartlett). This British Dykes Medal winner is a lovely flower. However, for me it has always grown as a short TB rather than a BB. For several years, I have crossed 'Orinoco Flow' with small BBs in an effort to produce a BB with the lovely plicata patterns, but in a true BB flower and plant. The line is progressing, although none have been suitable for introduction.

'Hillbilly Heaven' (Spahn). A lovely pink with ruffles and lace, it combines the last of the Fay and Hall tangerine lines, and both of these parents give small seedlings. 'Hillbilly Heaven' combines the best qualities of both lines and has

'Sheer Excitement' is Rick Tasco's vigorous luminata BB.

'Frosty Spirit' is one of the few really good pale-blue BBs currently available.

TOP 'Orinoco Flow' is really too big a flower and too tall a stalk for a proper BB, but it is lovely nevertheless and won the British Dykes Medal.

MIDDLE A seedling from 'Orinoco Flow' that has better BB proportions but is not good enough to introduce

BOTTOM 'Hillbilly Heaven' is a laced pink.

been a useful parent to produce BBs, because it is easily fertile and sets big pods.

'Marmalade Skies' (Niswonger). 'Marmalade Skies' is derived from Jean Stevens's classic TB cocoa-pink amoena 'Sunset Snows', which had small flowers and gave a preponderance of smaller flowers in its progeny. In 'Marmalade Skies' the colors are considerably cleaner (apricot-orange bicolor) and the stalks are in the BB range. 'Marmalade Skies' has been a great boon as a parent for BBs.

'Pebbles' (Tucker). Paul Cook produced the hybrid 'Wide World' derived from *I. imbricata*, one of the species that is of BB size. 'Pebbles' has pale-blue standards over white falls gently pebbled blue, and is a first-generation seedling from 'Wide World'. It was one of the first BBs I saw as a kid, and I fell in love with them forever.

'Pink Bubbles' (Hager). Ben Hager introduced a tall bearded pink named 'Beverly Sills' that went on to win the Dykes Medal. This clear-pink BB sister seedling takes the opera singer's nickname, Bubbles. This is a consistent BB and a great grower.

'Soft Spoken' (Dyer). The late Perry Dyer introduced many fine irises, but I go back to this true classic. It is always in-class, with stalks around 20 inches tall, and the flowers are always a perfect shade of soft lavender on beautifully branched stalk.

'Tulare' (Hamblen). Melba Hamblen was a close friend of breeder Tell Muhlestein and watched with interest his progeny from 'Golden Flash' × 'Yellow Dresden', which featured large rows of perfectly formed BBs. Using one of these seedlings in crosses, she produced this golden-yellow flower with orange beard and perfect BB proportions. It is in the lines of several modern BBs and still looks good despite its years.

And a couple of older diploids:

'Pink Ruffles' (Smith). When I was growing up in New England, this plant was in virtually every garden. A vigorous grower that produced a sea of pretty orchid flowers, it has made an impact on MTB breeding and is behind the Dunderman orchids and pink plicatas.

'Pretty Butterfly' (Sass). One of the last products of the Sass line, this plant features a pretty amoena pattern of white standards and purple falls. It has been an interesting parent crossed onto MTBs, resulting in progeny with fuller forms and bright colors.

'Network' (Witt). This was from a group of seedlings derived from the *I. variegata* var. *reginae* that had lots of striping in the flower. 'Network' adds that veining to the plicata pattern in deep purple. Always in-class and an eager grower, it is the perfect plant to add a little pizzazz to the perennial border.

New Favorites

'Banana Royale' (Aitken). Terry Aitken has been working a line of BBs descended from 'Brown Lasso' and various oranges for many years. He has pulled out many fine BBs in a wide range of colors, including reverse amoenas, oranges with banded fall patterns, and dark top combinations. 'Banana Royale' is a wonderful yellow infused with peach, with an orange beard.

'Banded Gold' and 'Banded Rose' (Aitken). These two are another generation of the Aitken line, offering clean, pretty flowers with distinct bands around the falls. It's amazing that such striking edges continue to appear, generations after 'Brown Lasso' was introduced into the gene pool.

'Devil's Waltz' (Markham). An appropriate name for this oddly colored flower that combines Lynn's line of dark BBs with the spooky TB blends of K eith Keppel. The result is a dark red / violet with almost gauze-like muting and contrasting bright-orange beards. 'Devil's Waltz' is a happy plant and grows extremely well in the South, something that dark irises don't often do.

'Dapple Dawn' (Markham). 'Dapple Dawn' is a complex blend of parentages, resulting in a bitone luminata on a strong lemon-yellow background. The background color seems to make the whole flower glow, and contrasts with the

TOP 'Pretty Butterfly' is a vigorous diploid BB that is a great plant for perennial borders.

BOTTOM The unusual blended gray-violet-purple 'Devil's Waltz'

pastel-lavender luminata pattern. 'Dapple Dawn' is a strong grower with lots of buds, and one of the first BBs to bloom here in Oregon.

'Preppy' (Vaughn). Its lavender pinstripes bring to mind that striped shirt worn by every preppy! It is a most reliable BB and a wonderful rebloomer in the South. There would often be a good clump in bloom at Christmastime when I lived in Mississippi. It has also turned out to be a valuable parent for BBs—in crosses with even TBs, most of the progeny are BBs. If you prefer luminata-plicatas to straight plicatas, its seedling 'See My Etchings' might be your choice. The habits are almost identical.

'Teapot Tempest' (Markham). What a happy camper this plant is! A lovely orchid purple with a blue beard that has great impact in the landscape. Its nicely proportioned flowers on well-branched stems ensure a long bloom period. This plant makes a beautiful clump year after year and is healthy as well. 'Teapot Tempest' has been one of my favorites since I saw it as a seedling in Lynn's garden.

'Venus Blush' (Black). 'Venus Blush' makes one of the most beautiful BB clumps I have ever seen. The flowers, stalks, and leaves are reduced in proportion, and the blooms at even the lowest positions open beautifully. The color is a little muted—a coppery peach—but the flaring, perky form and bright beard make the ensemble work. It is turning out to be an important parent for in-class BBs.

TOP The vigorous reblooming BB 'Preppy'

BOTTOM 'Venus Blush' is one of the most perfectly proportioned BBs.

REFERENCES

Jones, B. C. "Median Irises III: The Border Bearded." In *The World of Irises*. Edited by B. Warburton and M. Hamblen, 131–135. Kansas City, MO: American Iris Society, 1978.

Smith, M. "Intermediate Bearded Fertility Study, 2004." *Bulletin of the American Iris Society* 337 (2005): 74–82.

Wright, M. "Proposed Standards for Border Bearded Irises." *The Medianite* 8 (1967): 20–21.

Culture of Dwarf and Median Bearded Irises

Dwarf and median bearded irises represent some of the easiest garden plants. However, knowing a few tricks for planting and growing them will keep both the irises and the gardener happy.

Choosing a Site

The two considerations for choosing a site for bearded-iris culture have traditionally been sun exposure and drainage conditions. This is still true, but I've gardened in several areas of the country that required modifications of these rules.

When I lived in New England (Zone 4–5), most gardeners used raised beds to house their collection of bearded irises. Some were tastefully bordered by stone or brick to create a formal layout. The soil inside these beds was prepared well ahead of planting and consisted of "good garden loam," generally a sandy loam mixed with organics (peat, sawdust, or compost) and treated with a bit of lime. The bed was allowed to settle before planting. These raised beds created perfect growing conditions with good drainage and light, friable soil. Beds were kept away from trees so that they received maximum sun. Even there, I grew some of my irises in part shade to maximize the number of irises I could plant.

When I gardened in Mississippi (Zone 8), drainage was also an issue, and I raised the beds by 4–6 inches, but sun was not as important. In fact, my best growth occurred where I had high shade from trees that were limbed up, allowing ample filtered light and air circulation and moderating the hot summer temperatures. Another advantage was that the colors that often fade in full sun (bright yellows and golds) retained their colors beautifully. I could grow all the bearded irises, although the MDBs with more pumila blood were much less happy. BBs and IBs were especially good in that climate.

Here in Oregon (Zone 8 but different than the Zone 8 of Mississippi), the majority of my bearded-iris beds are in full sun, although several large beds are on a west-facing slope that doesn't receive sun until about 9 a.m. The hill provides drainage, so the beds are only 2–4 inches above the path. In the main garden, more-formal beds are made from pavers that raise the bed about 8 inches above the paths. Soil is a sandy loam with lots of organic material incorporated, and alfalfa meal and lime added to the mix. Part of the beds are over a former parking area where broken concrete and gravel provide alkaline feet for the irises. In all these situations, their growth is good.

When I moved to Oregon, I was horrified that many of my colleagues grew their irises in heavy clay. Some had ground that would make good clay pots! This went against my belief that silty soil was the irises' favorite. However, it turns out that irises really like the clay that covers much of the Willamette Valley. The beds are in full sun, and the irises are planted on ridges above the paths. The irises seem to enjoy the minerals in the soil, producing huge, gorgeous rhizomes.

I have seen some extreme plantings in climates that are less bearded-iris friendly. In humid Raleigh,

North Carolina, the late Loleta Powell grew bearded irises on the slopes of 4-foot berms. In a wet and humid climate, this ensured that the rhizomes stayed dry.

So, to summarize: In general, plant in raised beds or on a slope so that water doesn't puddle. Preferably, plant your irises in soil that has not seen irises previously. Place the beds toward full sun in northern climates but give them more shade as you move southward.

Planting

Nurseries ship irises in boxes with packing material that keeps the rhizomes dry. The foliage will be trimmed in an inverted V and ready for planting. Labels are either stapled to the leaves or wrapped around the iris fan. Be careful not to misplace them.

There are several schools of thought on planting. I was trained in the East Coast method that William McKee and Betty Nesmith used in their nurseries (Nesmith 1959). Two shallow holes are dug next to each other, and the rhizome is placed on the ridge between the holes. The roots are then spread into the adjoining shallow holes. Compost is added to the far edges of each hole (careful that it doesn't touch the rhizome), and then the soil is pulled back around the plants. The rhizome should be covered by ½–1 inch of soil for a BB or IB, less than that for the smaller irises. A good rule of thumb for planting depth is to make sure that all the green foliage is exposed above ground. Pat the soil to tighten it, and then water it in with a transplant fertilizer such as QuickStart™ until the soil is well wetted. Water every two to three days in the absence of rainfall until new growth is visible.

The West Coast method is easier and faster. Ben Hager (1978) described this quick technique. Dig a shallow hole, stretch the roots straight down, and make sure the rhizome isn't planted too deeply. Pull the soil back around the iris plant, give it some water, and move on. Ben had a commercial operation, and his method is obviously quick enough to plant thousands of rhizomes. It also works. His Melrose Gardens shipped some beautiful rhizomes. If I'm in a hurry, I'll use this method, but I mainly use the East Coast method. If I'm spending $25 on an SDB, I want to give it at least a $50 hole!

The old rule of thumb—planting bearded irises like "a duck on water" with some of the rhizome above the soil surface and some below—is no longer in vogue, although I find that iris clumps with the rhizomes tops exposed continue to thrive. Still, the chances for sun scalding the rhizomes are greater when the rhizome is exposed, so it is best to put some soil on these exposed rhizomes to keep them happy.

If you buy multiples of a dwarf or median, you can make a faux clump of irises. Plant them in an imaginary triangle with the fans at the corner and the toes of the rhizomes pointed inward or in one direction. Even in the first year, these faux clumps will look more like a two- or three-year clump.

No matter which planting method you choose, you will want to label the plants so that both you and garden visitors know what cultivars are planted where. I buy aluminum markers (from PawPaw Everlast Label Co.) in several sizes. The miniature ones are sized for MDBs and SDBs; the medium-sized ones are appropriate for the taller medians. Because my penmanship lacks some clarity, I use a label maker and waterproof labeling tape. The tape is rather pricey but lasts a long time. Plants that were labeled ten years ago when I moved to Oregon are still intact and readable. I have seen similar markers used in which the gardener's penmanship was quite beautiful, and the markers were an asset to the landscape. I'll let you decide where your penmanship falls in this continuum.

Planting distances vary with the type of iris. MDBs may be planted as close as 8 inches apart, whereas a foot or more is appropriate for the larger medians. The closer the irises are planted, the more immediate the effect, but also the sooner that digging and transplanting will be required. Some of the best iris culture I have ever observed is that of the late Kenneth Stone from Ashby, Massachusetts. He grew irises on 3-inch centers, and they were absolutely clean and the most perfect example of a cultivar I had ever seen. He also mulched his irises with a thin layer of white pine needles, which brings me to the discussion of mulch.

Traditionally, bearded irises are not mulched. Rather, a "dust mulch" is maintained by shallow cultivation to prevent weeds and keep the soil aerated. This is the practice in most of the iris gardens I have visited. If there is mulch, it is confined to the paths. Bee Warburton grew her irises in rows and, between the rows, used a heavy mulch of wood chips and with a light covering of pine needles on the irises. My mentor Polly Bishop used a thin mulch of buckwheat hulls directly on the bearded irises. They are a light mulch, so they breathe and then break down into organic matter useful for the plant and, at least in Polly's sandy soil, caused no rot issues. Here in the Pacific Northwest, I have seen hazelnut shells, which decompose slowly, as a mulch in beds, but more frequently in the pathways. Occasionally gravel is also used to mulch the plants. All of these are options if you are not happy with the plants that are grown unmulched.

Many growers use herbicides that disrupt weed seed germination or growth. The two most common ones are packaged in the Preen Plus™ herbicide. These inhibit either plant microtubules or cellulose biosynthesis (Vaughn 2000); they are relatively safe for gardeners because they inhibit plant-specific processes. They are relatively benign to irises and are especially effective at controlling grasses and small dicotyledon weeds that are major weed pests of irises. Preen Plus is applied by shaking the granules around the iris plants and then watering it in (or applying just prior to a good rain) so that it forms a crust that will stop the weed seeds from germinating or developing. I do find that there is some "root pruning" (inhibited root growth) if the herbicides are used too frequently. This root pruning seems to affect the MDBs and SDBs more than other bearded irises. The herbicides are effective for four to six months, depending on your climate.

I do not use nonselective herbicides or those that kill dicot weeds. I have had a little luck with either glyphosate or triclopyr solutions, using a fine and carefully directed spray. This is especially effective on deep-rooted perennial weeds, such as thistle, that are difficult to control with standard weeding practices. Irises are sensitive to these herbicides, and even small doses will cause stunted growth, loss of chlorophyll from the fans, white stripes on colored cultivars, and flower deformations. Be careful, and apply these herbicides only on absolutely still days.

Here in the Pacific Northwest, the climate is benign enough that irises need no winter protection. In colder areas a winter mulch is a good idea. The trick is to keep the soil frozen after it has frozen. It is the change of temperatures and subsequent heaving of the plants that is so destructive. Salt marsh hay is the traditional mulch, but evergreen boughs that are plentiful in November and December are a good substitute. The branches of discarded Christmas trees can be used as well. MDBs and SDBs, with their smaller rhizomes and root masses, are more prone to heaving. Placing a rock or brick over the rhizomes will slow the heaving. In Maine, many growers cover their plants with garden quilts. My only concern is that voles might find it a perfect winter retreat and use the irises as snacks.

Companion Plants

Although many irisarians grow beds of all irises, a much more interesting approach is to include a variety of perennials that complement the irises and extend the bloom season. My own garden is more of a "horticultural gumbo" with all sorts of plants thrown into the stew. For a bed of dwarfs and medians, smallish perennials with thin foliage and a similar culture are the perfect pick. Although some of these were brought in as companions, they have become favorites, and I now collect and hybridize these as well. The book *The Smaller Perennials* (Elliott 1997) contains lots of wonderful selections. Below are some of my favorites.

The many *Dianthus* cultivars, known collectively as pinks (Bird 1994), start blooming during iris season and offer a series of white, pink, and red flower colors, many with contrasting eyes or patterns, that look good with blue- and purple-toned iris flowers. The flowers have a delightful smell of cloves that has been bred out of the florist carnations but is retained in these miniature versions. Even when *Dianthus* are not blooming, the plants have gorgeous silver foliage that persists all season. My favorite cultivars include the singles 'Tyrian', 'Georgia Peach Pie', and 'Sops in Wine' and the semidoubles 'Rosebud', 'Jan Louise', and 'Double Bubble'. However, almost any of the cultivars are worth growing. *D. deltoides* is a rampant but charming and small-leaved species planted with the white with red-eye cultivar 'Arctic Fire'. Just watch it so that it doesn't engulf the irises.

Penstemons are wonderful North American natives, with cultivars ranging from several inches tall to a towering 3 feet (Way and James 1998). The smaller ones are, of course, best with the medians and dwarfs. The "shrubby penstemons" are some of the smallest despite their group collective name. These include hybrids from *P. rupicola*, *P. newberyi*, and *P. fruiticosus* in shades from white to blue lavender, and rosy pink. They have amusing tubular blossoms and stay in neat clumps. They start to bloom with late medians and continue for about a month.

A slightly taller group includes the Prairie series that were created at the University of Nebraska North Platte experiment station, such as the violet-blue 'Mesa', bright-red 'Prairie Fire', and soft-purple 'Prairie Dusk'. These plants make neat clumps with low rosettes of leaves, and stalks with an abundance of flowers. These are restrained perennials and bloom for a long time. A more recent development is the Mexicali hybrids created by Bruce Meyers. His ingenious crosses of northwestern US and Mexican species capture the hardiness and persistence of the northwestern US species and the beautiful colors and patterned throats from the Mexican species. Several clones have been selected from these lines, including 'Pikes Peak Purple' and 'Sunburst Amethyst'. The Mexicali series can get big, but they can be trimmed back or have their cuttings rooted. They also come easily from seed. The seedlings from these are similar to the parents, and all are useful garden plants.

Intriguing marking on the author's dianthus seedling

A mixture of penstemon seedlings of the author's, derived from the Prairie series

One other species that is easy for most areas of the country is *P. hirsutus*. The best forms of this plant are squatty and vary in color from clear white to a good purple. The plants are not as persistent as the other species mentioned, but they readily seed, and all the seedlings are garden-worthy. The American Penstemon Society has a wonderful seed exchange where improved selections of these species may be obtained. From what I've seen, there are almost no bad ones, and most are happy with bearded-iris culture.

Hardy succulents are lovely companions to the dwarf and median irises. The *Sempervivum* (commonly known as houseleeks or hens-and-chicks) are effective edging plants and come in a wide variety of colors and forms. If your raised beds are made of stone, the *Sempervivum* will gently spill down and about these stones, softening the edge of the bed. The smaller cultivars and species are best for edging beds of MDBs or SDBs; bigger ones can be used in bordering the taller medians. There are over 7,000 cultivars on the market, and some of the recent hybrids are gold, brilliant red, and dark purple verging on black. Textures vary from smooth and waxy to strongly hirsute. The so-called cobweb forms have hairs at the terminus of each leaf that connect to form a "web" that does resemble a cobweb. Cobweb types tend to make smaller rosettes, and the flowers are a cheerful rose red on short stalks, unlike some of the larger hybrids. I have bred many of these cultivars, and interested readers can consult my book on *Sempervivum* for more details (Vaughn 2018).

What was formerly the genus *Sedum* is now split into several genera, and most of the ones I like with irises are the clump-forming sorts that are now classified under *Hylotelephium*. Brent Horvath's wonderful book *The Plant Lover's Guide to Sedums* (Horvath 2014) details many of these. Chris Hansen's new Sunsparkler series of clumping sedums are an example of a new breed of sedums that have compact clumps, colorful foliage, and a long bloom season starting in late summer. Here in the Pacific Northwest, the native sedums *S. oreganum*, *S. spathulifolium*, and *S. laxum* are wonderful in combination with irises because they make low, spreading clumps that are never invasive. Unfortunately they are not happy in many other climates.

An unlikely companion to dwarf and median irises is the new generation of *Allium* (ornamental onion) hybrids. These clump-forming types from *A. senescens* and *A. cernuum* thrive under the conditions that bearded irises prefer, and the narrow, upright leaves, sometimes glaucous, are showy and neat. Blooms start in midsummer and go on to fall. *A.* 'Millenium' was one of the Perennial

Sempervivum 'Patent Leather Shoes' is one of the new generation of hybrids.

A cobweb-type *Sempervivum* of the author's

TOP Chris Hansen's Sunsparkler series of hardy sedums are all compact, clumping plants with wonderful foliage and a bouquet of flowers.

MIDDLE A dark-flowered *A. cernuum* seedling of the author's has an unusual assemblage of flowers.

BOTTOM The sprawling hardy geranium 'Ann Folkard' is a charming and bright addition to the iris garden.

Plant Association's plants of the year, and a good one to start with this genus because it's an easy grower. Other fun hybrids are 'Lavender Bubbles' and 'Blue Eddy', the latter with blue and somewhat twisted foliage. The species *A. cernuum* has charming, drooping flower heads with dark-purple flowers that look almost alien! Even the more common chive plant has nice lavender flowers and the added bonus of providing a few leaves for stews or salads. Cultivars and species that seed too much or produce bulbils on the flowering stem should be avoided (Davies 1992).

Hardy geraniums have gone through a breeding revolution in the last two decades, chiefly from our British hybridizers, and there are now lots of choice ones that can be grown with dwarf and median irises (Parer 2016). There are many fine cultivars of the low-spreading *G. sanguineum*, varying in color from white to all shades of pink and a shrieking magenta. This species is known as the "Bloody Cranesbill" because the fall foliage is bright red. My favorite cultivars are the white 'Pure Joy', pale-pink 'Appleblossom', and magenta-edged, near-white 'Elke'. Alan Bremner has produced many fine hybrids. One of his best is 'Joy', which makes low clumps of silver-green leaves and pale-pink flowers. 'Rozanne' seems to be everywhere and blooms for a long time, although I object some to its sprawling nature; make sure you keep the stems off the irises. Several sports from 'Rozanne' have been named that offer different shades and slightly different growth habits. Of these sports, my current favorite is 'Azure Rush', which is more compact than 'Rozanne'. For a brighter color, the scrambling 'Ann Folkard' has amazing flowers of screaming magenta with a black eye.

A couple of the other irises also make excellent companions to the dwarfs and medians. The recent selections of the miniature bulbous iris *I. reticulata*, especially those hybridized by Alan McMurtrie, are wonderful garden plants. In Oregon, these bloom in February and March and finish just as the MDBs' blooms begin. Plant these bulbs in clumps and drifts along the edges of beds. Less

well-known irises that grow well in beds of bearded irises are the forms of *I. tectorum*, the so-called roof iris. The white form (*alba*) is especially attractive, but none of these are ugly, and they make neat, 12–18-inch-tall clumps of bloom. I find that most of the beardless irises don't mix as well with the dwarfs and medians, because they are too big or require more moisture, shade, or acidic conditions. I do use some spuria irises at the back of mixed beds, and the small spuria species *I. graminea* and *I. sintenissii* in the foreground with the dwarfs and medians.

Medians and dwarfs bloom at about the same time as many popular spring bulbs. Daffodils are such cheery flowers, and I grow lots of them, but in general not with the irises. Their problem is the dying foliage, which cannot be trimmed away without damaging their growth. The Division 6 *cyclamineus* hybrids have much-smaller and much-lower foliage and come in a wide range of colors, blooming about the same time as the MDBs. Some of these, such as 'Rapture', have an amusing form that complements and contrasts with the iris bloom. There are also a number of really fine miniature daffodils that fit in perfectly and often bloom with the earliest MDBs. Tulips have wonderful clear reds that make irises envious. Here in Oregon, the SDBs and IBs bloom during the same season as the tulips and are excellent companions. Tulip foliage also degrades, but it isn't quite as messy as the larger daffodils and still looks good as the irises are blooming. The species tulips

Tulips are a pleasant companion to dwarf irises in Michele Shriber's garden.

in bright colors and with smaller flowers look especially good mixed with dwarfs and medians. I find cool tones in the irises are best to set off the tulip colors, although some of the gaudy yellows mixed with red tulips make for an outrageous combination.

Miniature and small-flowered daylilies are attractive companion plants to dwarf and median irises because they have the same reduced proportions relative to their bigger relatives as the dwarf and median irises do. Size in daylilies is determined solely by the bloom diameter, with miniatures defined as those less than 3 inches in diameter, and small-flowered between 3 and 4.5 inches in diameter (Vaughn 2002). Thus, when picking varieties to go with the medians and dwarf, you may want to choose varieties that are shorter as well as small flowered. Ben Hager introduced a couple of "micro-minis" such as 'Penny's Worth' and 'Penny Earned', with scapes no taller than 8 inches and flowers about 1 inch in diameter. A number of the "little yellow varmint" types such as 'Bitsy', 'Stella d'Oro', and 'Happy Returns' start to bloom just as the irises are ending, and rebloom for much of the growing season. Elizabeth Salter and Grace Stamile have produced outstanding small and miniature daylilies in intriguing colors and patterns from white to dark purple, including some with respectable blue eyes. You don't have to rely on old 'Stella d'Oro' anymore for your small daylily choice. Several small double daylilies create a totally different effect because they don't look like other daylilies. The dainty, cascading clumps of miniature daylily foliage are a nice contrast in form to the irises too.

The author's miniature daylily seedling with a blue eye

A number of annuals work well with irises. Pansies are one of my favorites because they provide wonderful winter color in temperate parts of the country and are still blooming as the irises begin to bloom in the spring. My mentor, Polly Bishop, crossed little Johnny jump-ups (*Viola tricolor*) with pansies to create a strain of smaller-flowered but easily self-seeding plants. These were so prolific that they created a "living mulch" around the irises, negating the need for more-extensive mulching and protecting the plant from heaving in winter. Even Bee Warburton, who grew irises in rows, loved the Johnny jump-ups growing among the irises, and selected a strain without the usual orange patch, which she found too jarring against the purple of the remainder of the flower.

The Rock Garden

Unless you are the kind of rock gardener who dismisses hybrids as not appropriate for a rock garden, MDBs and SDBs are perfect for this use. Pure *pumila* cultivars are, in fact, pure species; they look marvelous intercalated between rocks and come in a nice variety of colors. Irises, especially dwarf ones, look marvelous around rocks, and they will relish the cool and moist soil under the rocks. Moreover, most delicate rock garden plants are perfect foils for MDBs and SDBs. Some of the smaller MTBs and IBs are also delicate enough to fit in.

The Mixed-Sun Border

Most gardeners are not iris fanatics but would like to have a few in the mixed border. In this case,

Two views of Michele Shriber's rock garden bedecked with MDBs and SDBs

some of the older classic diploid BBs work nicely. I would also add most of the diploid MTBs because they are vigorous enough to stand competition from other plants. Some of the IBs, especially heavy rebloomers such as 'Constant Companion', can work well too. Even in these situations, be sure the irises are not covered up by their neighbors. Irises need to get light down to the rhizome to make flowers for the next season.

Edging these beds with SDBs or MDBs also works well, given the above caveats. Here again, reblooming SDBs offer some of the best plants for the more rough-and-tumble situations of the mixed-sunny border.

I grew up admiring Miriam Corey's Massachusetts garden. Her beds were backed by stone walls (and even a huge boulder). They were 8 feet deep and several hundred feet in length. These spacious beds had broad sweeps of TB irises, peonies, Oriental poppies, and daylilies—plants that have a big presence and take up lots of room. Constructing a garden like this requires lots of space, and few gardeners could pull off that look today. However, a much-narrower and less extensive border could be created that uses both medians and dwarfs for the foreground and middle. A few taller perennials in the back, such as TB irises, asters, helenium, and garden phlox, would create a beautiful picture.

Narrow Borders and Spot Gardens

We all have those areas where there is a small area of land, maybe next to a shed or a patio, that is not big enough to create a full garden but would look good with a few plants. Here the dwarfs and medians could be used to great effect. I especially like MTBs for this situation because they make tight clumps with lots of flowers. Planted close to the house, they could be a good source for bouquets. They also tolerate shade better than most other bearded irises, and these leftover spaces tend to be next to structures such as sheds and garages that block the sun.

The Schreiners have a huge (7-acre) display garden that shows how irises can be used as landscape plants. Although most of the beds are devoted to TBs, they devoted a long, narrow strip at the edge of the garden to medians and dwarfs in huge clumps. This strip, several feet wide, is a solid mass of bloom for weeks and is an extremely effective demonstration of the use of medians and dwarfs.

Pots

Although the tall bearded irises are really not acceptable for pot culture because of their size and root run, almost all the dwarfs and medians are. With so many gardeners working with small yards, pots of dwarfs and medians are a great way to grow a collection of iris in a confined space. My friend Lynn Smith has developed one of the cleverest ways to use of MDBs and SDBs. She grows *Sempervivum* in raised beds that have been constructed from cement blocks. This left an edging of open holes in the cement blocks that Lynn filled in with soil, leaving little planters for the dwarf irises. The dwarfs excelled in these little holes and were a marvelous accent to her *Sempervivum* collection.

Water and Fertilizer

I was brought up with the idea that too much water could only lead to rot, and that may be true in a climate where the summers tend to be wet and humid. Even in Massachusetts we had summer droughts, and the irises needed less than what most other plants required. If you wanted rebloom of any kind, watering was a must. When I gardened in Mississippi, however, summer rainfall was often abundant because of daily thunderstorms and high humidity. I probably watered the bearded irises fewer than a dozen times in twenty-five years, other than when I was planting a new bed.

In Oregon, we have a dry summer (in great contrast to our winters), and I water the bearded-iris plantings twice a week to keep the ground moist but not sopping. This took some mental adjustment after not watering established bearded iris in the summer in two previous climates.

However, the foliage and rate of increase are really superior to those unwatered areas where the foliage looks old and withered. On hot days, it is essential to water the beds early in the morning or late in the evening, never in the heat of the day.

Fertilizer is needed two times during the year for optimal performance when the plants are working extra hard to develop either blooms or increase. I sprinkle about a half cup of fertilizer around (not on) each clump about six weeks before peak bloom in the spring and four to six weeks after bloom in the summer, around half the dose of the spring fertilizing. I try to do at least the spring fertilizing right before a rain (that's easy here in Oregon), and I water after the summer fertilizing. Each time, I use a granular 5-10-10 fertilizer and have done so in Massachusetts and Mississippi too. Irises definitely need potassium and potash, but nitrogen can send the growth into overdrive, promoting foliage rather than flowers. However, different soils have different deficiencies, and it is good to have a soil test conducted, especially if you see reduced growth. My friend in Texas, Judy Schneider, has told me that 5-10-10 is not a good fertilizer regime for her because the soil needs more nitrogen and less of the other two.

ABOVE Lynn Smith's planting of dwarf irises in holes created in cement blocks filled with soil

In addition to the chemical fertilizers, I treat the beds with alfalfa pellets or meal (Aitken 1996). Rose growers were the first to recognize the use of alfalfa in promoting plant growth, but iris growers also recognize its value. Besides adding alfalfa around the clumps, I incorporate a bale in each of the 6-by-25-foot seedling beds, and proportionately more to new or reworked beds. Likewise, I will use some composted cow manure when planting new bearded iris, but I'll also add a bale of composted cow manure when remaking the beds. Chad Harris, who grows some of the most perfect iris on the planet, swears by cow manure for keeping his planting fields fresh. Both alfalfa and composted manures are safe additions to the soil. Some growers have declared alfalfa pellets a miracle, enabling irises to grow even in worn-out soil. Alfalfa contains triacontanol, which has been shown to stimulate growth in other plants, but it may merely be supplying nitrogen and minerals that irises need.

About every other year I sprinkle ground lime around the iris clumps, and a little less right in the center of the clump. Bearded irises prefer neutral to basic soil, and in Oregon we have naturally acidic soil. You might not need this if you live in areas with higher-pH soil than mine. What the lime does is make nutrients available to the plants, and it also supplies the calcium that plants require. Most bearded irises grow fine in a range of pHs from 6 to 8, although at the high end you may notice some reduced growth.

Bearded iris are heavy feeders and do tend to wear out the soil. Commercial growers rotate their iris fields to prevent this from happening. But small-time gardeners can't afford this fallow space. I keep a pile of new soil, and any clump over two years old is top- and side-dressed with fresh soil—at a half inch in the middle of the clump and some on the sides. This treatment allows me to keep a clump longer before transplanting. When planting a new iris in an existing bed, I dig out the soil that grew the old iris and replace it with new soil.

Eventually, though, a clump will have to be dug and divided. Using a strong spading fork, lift the clump and free it from the soil. Now examine the clump. The old, nearly dead rhizomes should be cut out of the clump with a knife and discarded. It is unlikely that they will produce good bloom, but if it is a particularly rare cultivar I might be tempted to keep these pieces to see if anything does mature. Now pick out the three best rhizomes to keep. Mother Nature plants in odd numbers, so three or five is a good amount to replant. Trim the leaves in an inverted V, leaving about half of the foliage intact. The trimming will decrease plant shock and transpiration. If you want to restore a clump effect quickly, make an imaginary triangle and plant the three rhizomes 6–8 inches apart (a bit more for BBs), with the toes of the rhizomes facing into the center. Water with a transplant fertilizer every few days until new shoot growth is noted.

Although bearded irises may be left out of the ground for a period of time, I almost always transplant MDBs the same day they are dug. This is especially important for the MDBs with more *pumila* blood. They have much-smaller rhizomes than the other classes, and thus fewer reserves to grow back their foliage and set blooms for the next season. That is one reason I do the top- and side-dressing technique to extend the period before transplanting. I have also simply cut a wedge out of a clump and moved the whole mass to a new location.

Maintaining Your Irises

There are a few simple rules for keeping your irises happy. Always trim with shears or clippers rather than pulling on the plants. The only dead leaves I remove without shears are those that are totally brown and pull away easily. If they resist pulling at all, I cut them off. Although all the irises have roots that are fairly well anchored, any pulling is likely to dislodge some of the roots and set the plant back. I always cut off the stalks after blooming. If you don't, they can go mushy and serve as a point of entry for rot. Besides, dead stalks just look bad!

Keep the area around your irises clear. This applies to companion plants as well as weeds. Weeds are efficient at robbing your irises of the nutrients they deserve. Moreover, rhizomes shaded by weeds or other plants won't ripen properly and bloom the following season.

Resist trimming back the foliage. Even though your irises arrived from the nursery trimmed in an inverted V, that process is to slow down transpiration during the shipping and replanting process. The foliage is providing much-needed fixed carbon to the plant. I trim only foliage that is brown or diseased. The diploid MTBs die to the ground, making for easy fall cleanup.

When I receive a box of rhizomes from a nursery, I do a little "preventative soak" in 5 percent Clorox for fifteen minutes. The plants are then washed with a stream of water from a hose and planted. This ensures that no pathogens from the nursery will make it to your garden.

Diseases and Pests

If you follow the rules of sun and drainage, you will eliminate many diseases. However, here are some common disease problems, their symptoms, and methods for control.

Leaf spot (*Didymellina macrospora*) is one of the most common of all iris diseases and is never lethal, although it is certainly disfiguring and probably reduces the plant's vigor. Generally leaf spot occurs during rainy periods. In the Pacific

Northwest, the worst infections are in the fall and winter, but in other areas it is more common in hot and humid summer months. The symptoms are round to oval spots that coalesce into a whole area, generally the tip, turning brown. What I have found most effective is to trim away as much of the affected areas as possible and then treat the entire planting with a fungicide such as Zineb or Maneb. There are several products that contain these or similar active ingredients.

Bacterial leaf blight looks similar to leaf spot, but the results are more severe. The spots are bigger and more irregular and occupy mostly the top third of the leaf. This was a problem when I grew irises in Massachusetts, but I have not seen it since moving to Mississippi and Oregon. Sanitation is the best control. Cut off the infected areas and burn them. Sometimes moving the irises to fallow areas after trimming can break the cycle.

Bacterial soft rot is caused by *Erwinia carotovora* and is one of the most insidious diseases of bearded iris. Once you smell the foul odor coming from an infected rhizome, you will never mistake it for anything else. One of the first signs of a problem is leaves falling away. Close inspection will reveal a soft area at the rhizome-leaf interface. If you catch it early, dig up the rhizome and scoop out the rotten areas of rhizome. Allow the rhizome to dry out, exposed to the sun. I also dust the rhizome with Comet or a similar cleanser. If a clump shows traces of rot, an application of Dial soap (which has the antibacterial triclosan) is a good treatment. In fact, I keep a huge bottle of it in the yard so I can treat anything suspect. Poor drainage and wet conditions invite soft rot. Wounds or insect damage often provide an entry point for bacteria.

Bearded-iris mosaic virus probably infects all bearded irises, but over time we have selected for clones that at least resist the symptoms. They are especially obvious during cool and rainy weather, so they disproportionately affect the earliest irises. Mild symptoms include mottled leaves; in advanced cases the blossoms are streaked with a darker anthocyanin or, alternatively, have clear patches or crinkled petals. These occur as sectors in the flower (Barnett 1972), similar to some of the broken color patterns.

Although mustard seed fungus is more of a problem for spuria irises, there are reports of it on bearded irises as well. Spuria irises are the canary in the coal mine; they are so sensitive that if I see any damage (either the webbing of the mycelium or the mustard seed–like fruiting bodies), I proactively treat all my irises with Terachlor. It is a nasty disease, and you do not want it. Luckily I have not seen this in my yard in Oregon.

Scorch is a strange disease because it can affect a single plant, leaving neighboring plants unscathed. Both leaves and roots rot or, more accurately, decay, while the rhizome stays intact. One of the treatments is to expose the rhizome to high temperatures, simply by drying it in the sun. Although originally a *Pseudomonas* was suspected as the causative agent, it is now more likely that mycoplasma-like organisms (MLOs) are responsible for the disease—they have been detected in the vascular system of scorched irises. Scorch spreads through sucking insects such as aphids, so controlling them is one way to limit infection.

Here in the West we have few bearded-iris insect pests, although cucumber beetles are good at eating the internal parts of the flowers. They are more prevalent later in the season and thus are especially damaging to reblooming irises. In the Midwest and on the East Coast, the iris borer is a serious problem. Its native host was probably the eastern blue flag, *I. versicolor*, and proximity to swamps where it grows seems to be correlated with damage. The iris borer is a moth that lays its eggs in and around clumps of iris. The borer emerges in the spring and works itself into the iris foliage. At this point, if you are observant, you can see finely abraded leaf edges. If you pull the fan open at the position of these abraded leaves, you will most often discover the borer, a whitish to tan caterpillar. Borers are generally solitary, so if you kill it, the problem will go away. When the borer invades the rhizome, the plant responds by shedding leaves or turning yellow.

Carefully remove irises with these symptoms and search for the borer. If you want to save the rhizome, give it a good cleaning with a 5 percent Clorox solution and replant. Often these wounded rhizomes will shoot out lots of increase.

The verbena bud moth is a problem for hybridizers. These annoying insects burrow into seed pods, and its invasion can usually be detected by a small hole at the base of the pod. The caterpillars enter the pod and begin devouring the immature seeds. Even the seeds that remain are contaminated. The most effective control is to cover the young capsule with scraps of panty hose or muslin, denying the moth access to the pod. The only problem is that this protection can cause moisture to accumulate, rotting the pod.

Deer do not favor bearded irises. However, they will take a sample bite here and there, and they seem to have a perverse sense of humor, chomping on your best new seedling or the cultivar you are waiting anxiously to see bloom. They can do more damage with their feet, stomping and damaging plants, although this is not lethal. I decided I didn't need deer in my garden, and installed an 8-foot deer fence. Problem solved.

Slugs are a way of life here in the Pacific Northwest, and irises are not immune to their effects. They have decimated whole MDB clumps in my garden. The trick is to start treating for them early. In Oregon, it starts in February, when the vegetation begins to grow in earnest. I use several kinds of slug bait. All are effective. Of course, the old "beer in the pie plate" method works pretty well, although my neighbor's cat is also fond of this.

I am sure voles are the devil's invention. These annoying rodents cause problems in several ways. When they burrow under your plantings, whole clumps of irises sink in the ground. And while bearded irises are not their favorite plant, they will chomp on Siberian irises with great relish. Mouse traps baited with peanut butter and placed near vole holes are useful in deterring these pests. A good fall garden cleanup is effective too; they tend to stay away from barren areas.

REFERENCES

Aitken, T. "Alfalfa: The Magic Elixir of Plant Life." *Bulletin of the American Iris Society* 303 (1996):45–46.

Barnett, O. W. "Viruses of Iris." *Bulletin of the American Iris Society* 205 (1972): 27–31.

Bird, R. *Border Pinks*. London: Batsford, 1994. 174 pp.

Davies, D. *Alliums: The Ornamental Onions*. Portland, OR: Timber, 1992. 168 pp.

Elliott, J. *The Smaller Perennials*. Portland, OR: Timber, 1997. 176 pp.

Hager, B. "Culture and Propagation." In *Garden Irises*. Edited by B. Warburton and M. Hamblen, 314–323. Wichita, KS: American Iris Society, 1978.

Horvath, B. *The Plant Lover's Guide to Sedums*. Portland, OR: Timber, 2014. 230 pp.

Nesmith, E. "Iris Culture in the Northeast." In *Garden Irises*. Edited by F. Randolph, 56–58. Ithaca, NY: Cayuga, 1959.

Parer, R. *The Plant Lover's Guide to Hardy Geraniums*. Portland, OR: Timber, 2016. 258 pp.

Vaughn, K. C. "Anticytoskeletal Herbicides." In *Plant Microtubules: Potential for Biotechnology*. Edited by P. Nick, 193–205. Berlin: Springer Verlag, 2000.

Vaughn, K. C. "Miniature and Small-Flowered Daylilies." In *The New Daylily Handbook*. Edited by F. Gatlin and J. R. Brennan, 145–168. Kansas City, MO: American Hemerocallis Society, 2002.

Vaughn, K. C. *Sempervivum: A Gardener's Perspective of the Not-so-Humble Hens-and-Chicks*. Atglen, PA: Schiffer, 2018. 208 pp.

Way, D., and P. James. *The Gardener's Guide to Growing Penstemons*. Portland, OR: Timber, 1998. 160 pp.

8

Hybridizing Dwarf and Median Bearded Irises

As you look through the photos of amazing dwarf and median irises in this book, consider that all but the species flowers exist because humans played plant matchmaker, creating something new in the world. Although one might consider the process daunting, if I could do it at age nine with no genetics training (albeit under careful tutelage), you can too.

Hybridizing bearded iris, or at least growing them from seed, is not new. Over four hundred years ago, Carolius Clusius observed that "irises grown from seed vary in a wonderful way." That variability is responsible for the spectacular development of bearded irises, with a color range from white to black and sizes from 3 inches to 4 feet. Initially, hybridizers saved seed pods from the bees and then selected desirable progeny, but by the early 1900s most of the hybridizers were making hand-crosses. It has been a revolution since then.

Hybridizing ornamental plants is a mix of science and art and imagination. When I make a cross, I have in my mind what the combination of the two parents might produce. As a beginner, you might start by crossing blues with blues or pastel colors with each other. From these sorts of crosses you generally get seedlings that are attractive, if not earth shattering, and often they are improvements on their parents. A quick read through the genetics section toward the end of this chapter might be a good idea before attempting that first cross. I also recommend Kenneth Kidd's genetics chapter in *The World of Irises* (1978) for a discussion of basic genetic principals.

Mechanics of Crossing

Examining a bearded-iris flower, one is at first confused about the location of the sexual apparatus. Many people assume that the beard is involved. It is not. To understand an iris flower, first remove the standards and falls. Neither has a role in pollination other than to attract insect pollinators. What you are left with are styles and stamens, the female and male parts of the plant, respectively. On the style is a little appendage of tissue, the stigmatic lip, where pollen is received. Early on in the opening of the flower, the stigmatic lip is tightly appressed to the rest of the style but gradually pulls away as the style becomes receptive to pollen.

The stamen consists of a filament (stalk) and the pollen-bearing anther. Two sutures on the anthers break open to allow the pollen to dehisce. In fertile varieties, the anthers will have a good quantity of pollen, colored from white to deep blue.

My pollination method is a variation on what was described earlier (Vaughn 2015). A flower just about to open (a bud that has cracked open just at the top) has its falls removed to stop bees and other insects from reaching the stigma. Even if the stigmatic lip has not opened, I take pollen from the chosen pollen parent and, using fine (Dumont #5) tweezers, I force pollen into the stigmatic lip. Even though the stigma is probably not receptive at that moment, as soon as it is, the pollen begins to germinate, ensuring pollination. Generally, I pollinate just one stigma because the

pollen can reach all three cavities in the ovary, and full pods of seed are the result. I often use anthers where the pollen has not dehisced. Using the point of the Dumont #5 tweezers, I run it along the suture line and ream the pollen out, collecting a portion on the tips of the tweezers. The pollen is sticky at this point, and I force it into the stigmatic lip. I have a similar success rate with pollen that has dehisced. If the pollen has already dehisced, I use the entire stamen and swipe the pollen on the stigmatic lip, pulling the lip down with a spare finger. For a while, I thought I was the only one using this technique on bearded irises, but I read a report from hybridizer Grace Guenther, who had been doing that since the 1950s (Guenther 1968).

Pollen may be stored for later use. I pick whole stamens and let them dry on a windowsill in my kitchen. As soon as the pollen has dehisced, I transfer the pollen to glassine envelopes that have been labeled with the iris name. I use a small jar that has a bit of silica gel at the base, and place it in the refrigerator. Anthers stored in this manner ensure viable pollen to use throughout the season. I collect more pollen than I use, but it is better to be overprepared for crosses than to wish you had saved pollen of a specific cultivar.

Traditionally, paper-stringed price tags were used to mark a cross, and many breeders still use that method. Many years ago, when visiting daylily friends in Florida, I learned of a method using small pieces of colored wire to mark a cross. It is what I use now. There are many colors of this wire, and daylily-hybridizing supply companies offer bundles of these in dozens of colors. Because I often repeat the same cross dozens of times, I can mark all those flowers with the same color of wire, saving time. In my notebook I'll record something like "'Alaia' × 'Droid', red wire" (parentages are always listed as pod parent × pollen

A bearded-iris flower on which the standards and falls are removed prior to crossing

parent). The wires are impervious to the weather, and the information on the cross is in my notebook, rather than on a tag that may be caked with mud by the time the cross is harvested. I use cheap bound school notebooks for recording this information and always write in pencil, so that if the notebook gets wet in the garden, the words are still legible. Moreover, the wire doesn't collect moisture in or around the pollinated flower, as paper tags often do, and the wires are more inconspicuous, so they don't mar the look of the plant.

I find it useful to carry all my crossing equipment in a little plastic basket with a handle. Here I keep tweezers, my notebook, a variety of crossing wires, several pencils, and some fine clippers to cut away flower parts. Others use aprons with multiple pockets.

If your cross is successful, the ovary will begin to swell in a few days, and in seven to ten days it will be an obvious pod (if it has taken). At that point it is wise to carefully remove other flowers in the same socket and to peel back the spathes that surround the flower base. They can collect water and rot the pod. In six to eight weeks the pod turns from green to brownish and begins to split at the tip. This is the time to collect the seeds, because the capsule will begin to disintegrate and seed will spill from the capsule. So, when pods begin to mature, you want to make daily garden rounds to check for ripening pods. Once the capsule splits, locating the seed on the ground is no easy task!

TOP A green pod, the result of a successful cross

BOTTOM A mature pod ready to be harvested

To Bee or Not to Bee?

I like to think I'm smarter than a bee in terms of selecting parents. Have I planted the occasional bee pod? Yes, especially when a parent has resisted my efforts at setting a pod on it. In the early days of MTB breeding, we were encouraged to save every pod on 'Pewee', and, in many years, the only seeds set on the MTBs were the few the bees had set. In 1970, almost no MTB set seed as a result of my hand-crosses, but I did harvest all the bee set seed and raised three hundred seedlings. It was a good thing, because 'Real Jazzy' and 'Little Bluebeard' came from those seeds. Today, I can't imagine doing that; the MTBs set many bee seed here, and my crosses take at about 80 percent most years. However, I have had no luck setting pods on 'Breakfast in Bed', despite crossing every flower for three years now. If a bee set a pod on it, I might be tempted.

If you are a beginner, bee pods are a good training tool for how to raise seedlings before growing seedlings from your careful hand-crosses. The Species Iris Group of North America and the British Iris Society offer seeds of bearded species and hybrids that can be used to learn techniques of seed germination and seedling culture. You are also supporting a good cause.

Growing Dwarf and Median Irises from Seed

After you harvest your seed from careful cross, your fun and work have just begun. The following protocols work for me here in Oregon, and I have used similar protocols when I lived in Massachusetts and Mississippi.

I dry my seeds in small plastic "weigh boats" that are used in scientific laboratories to weigh out chemical reagents on balances. I choose ones with fairly tall sides so I don't spill out the seeds from the cross; pill boxes or other open containers also work fine. I write the cross on these boats with a Sharpie so the cross is marked as the seed is drying (the Sharpie markings can be removed with ethanol, so the weight boats may be reused from year to year). You just want the seeds to get rid of any excess moisture so that they don't mold. Any other open container that breathes also works well. In the past I have used paper bags, pill boxes, and matchboxes. After three or four weeks of drying, these seeds are stored in coin envelopes until planting. At that point, I record all the successful crosses in my hardbound notebook and assign each cross an alphanumeric code. So the 2016 crosses were year Y, my twenty-fifth year of crossing irises after a hiatus of a few years during graduate school. Each cross has a number, so cross Y01 is the cross of two MDBs, 'Black Olive' × 'Chemistry'. When I started out, I had a complicated system of abbreviated parents' names, but that quickly became unwieldy as the pedigrees became more complex.

Here in Salem, Zone 8, I plant my seed from late September through mid-October. This ensures that I have good weather for the planting, but the planting is not so early that the seed germinates early and has to be protected over the winter. I use a commercial potting soil in 6-inch pots, dividing the seed into more than one pot if there are large numbers. In that case, divide the seed lot into twenty-five to thirty seeds per pot. For a marker, I use aluminum labels and write the cross and seed lot number on the tag with a #2 pencil. These labels follow the germinating seedlings to the seedling bed, serving as a marker all the way to blooming. I fill the pot three-quarters of the way to the top of the pot, put the seeds in a layer, and cover them with less than an inch of potting soil. The soil is then firmed and watered thoroughly. The pots are placed in two graveled areas outside my garage, mostly protected from winter freezes but exposed to cold and rain. The winter rains leach the germination inhibitors from the seed coat, and the seedlings start to germinate in March in Oregon, beginning with the MDBs and ending with the BBs and TBs. If a freeze is forecast after the seedlings have begun to germinate, I cover the pots with Remay, which protects them down to 22 degrees F. If lower temperatures are forecast, the pots make a move to the garage. No sense losing a year of crossing to the weather. Make sure the pots are moist if you find yourself in a winter dry spell.

Breeders use a couple of different treatments to improve germination. One is a good soak before planting. Transfer the seeds to paper cups or the weighing boats used for seed drying, and cover the seeds with water. Let them soak for twenty-four hours and then plant as described above. For seeds that are particularly difficult to germinate seeds (such as those of recessive amoenas), it is profitable to nick the seeds with a razor blade or to use fine sandpaper to abrade the seed coat.

Some crosses do not germinate the first year, so I keep those pots over one more year if nothing appears the first year. I either keep these pots moist or put them in shady portions of the yard where summer watering is likely to occur.

When the seedlings are 1 or 2 inches tall and all danger of frost has passed, I transplant the seedlings to raised beds. This is earlier than many of my colleagues, but I find that small seedlings, often with seed still attached, fare better than bigger plants, and the earlier transplanting gets them into the seedling bed before temperatures get too high. For seedling beds, I use raised beds that have been worked the fall before and new topsoil added to raise the beds 4 to 8 inches. The beds range from 4 to 6 feet wide and up to 25 feet long. I plant much more densely than most, with 4 inches between each seedling and 4–6 inches between the rows—a bit wider for BBs. Because my seedlings bloom almost 100 percent in one year, I can use this close spacing. The seedlings are watered in with a transplant fertilizer such as Quick Start, and that fertilizer dose is repeated every week until early September. After that time, the seedlings are allowed to harden off. Growth is quite amazing. From a few tiny green shoots in May, by August most of the seedlings have increase. Seedlings require a constant source of moisture during this rapid growth; mine are watered every third day if there is no rain.

Excitement is high as the new seedlings begin to bloom. It is like opening presents on Christmas morning, but better because you've had a hand in their creation. Your first reaction might be to love them all, but sanity soon prevails and you realize that there are both good and poor seedlings in the patch. One of the best friends of a hybridizer is a big discard pile! Noted daylily hybridizer Pauline Henry was ruthless in her selections. Any seedling that had a "bad hair day" was eliminated with a machete chop! This worked; her hybrids had good, consistent flowers and are behind several other lines.

Keep these criteria in mind when selecting new seedlings:

Color: Clear colors and patterns are favored. Breakthroughs such as significantly better red or blue colors should be saved, regardless of other deficiencies. Beard colors may be harmonious or clashing.

Form: Wide petals with horizontally flaring falls are preferred on small irises; a semiflared posture is acceptable in BBs and taller IBs. Standards may be domed or slightly open but must be firmly held.

Substance: A flower should last three days under normal conditions. Flimsy flowers that lose their shape are tossed out without a second thought.

Proportion: The size of the flower should be proportionate to the height of the stalk. The stalk must arise above the foliage, and the foliage should not be too wide or tall.

Distinction: Looking "just like something else" is no reason to keep a seedling. Keepers must be an improvement on their parents.

Vigor: Four increases is my line in the sand for an adequate increaser here in Oregon, but of course more are always better.

Buds and branching: This varies with different classes. MDBs can have as few as one bud, although at least two is preferred, and three for SDBs, five for IBs, and seven or more for BBs and MTBs. Branches should not crowd flowers to the stem, nor be too ungainly.

Seedlings stalks are tagged with a plastic marker with the seedling number. An orange pin flag like

A bed of median seedlings four months after planting

those used on construction sites is inserted into the clump to facilitate finding the selected seedlings when they need to be dug. The flags have thin stakes and can be put close to the seedling.

You have some paperwork to do too. In your notebook write a brief description that includes details of height, and size and color of the flowers. I use the alphanumeric generated when I plant the seed, so that the first seedling selected from cross Y01 is numbered Y01-1. These records are invaluable later when plants are being registered. Digital images are also obtained. Others use a system of year and number of the selected seedling, such as 02-21 for the second seedling marked in 2021. This requires less planning ahead, and many major hybridizers used this method. Whatever your system, record it in your notebook. Even careful hybridizers lose records, or markers are moved by accidents. One year I had a garden visitor with a small child who, left unattended, picked up a whole handful of labels from my seedling bed! Luckily I had mapped the bed in my notebook.

Let's talk about notebooks. The notebook where I record my crosses and seedlings is a bound book. I write only on the right-hand pages, leaving the left page blank to note things that might be confusing, such as numbers switched or a parent that might not be the one listed based on the progeny. This goes to the garden only when I'm recording new seedlings, and is recorded in pen. A second notebook is my daily crossing book—a small, bound school-type book in which I record everything in pencil. I start each day of crossing on a new page. I list the crosses I've made each day and what color wire marks the cross. After a cross has taken, I put a big check mark next to it. This makes harvesting the pods less of a chore, because you know what pods should be ripe and on what cultivars.

A looser type of pad is used to construct a map of the seedling planting. This map is constructed as the seedlings are being rowed out, and is written in pencil, because I frequently bring it to the field as seedlings are blooming. In Oregon, frequently that is a rainy day, and pencil doesn't run or smear. In years past, I have laminated these sheets. A third small notebook, also bound, sits on my nightstand near my bed. This was inspired after reading the notebooks of MTB pioneers Jean Witt and Alice White. They talked to themselves in their notebooks with comments like "Need to cross yellows into reds this season" and "Why didn't I repeat this cross?" In my notebook, I jot down what crosses to complete during the next season, which lines to keep exploring and which to drop, and which new plants in my garden might be added to existing lines. During bloom season, I read this notebook before going to the yard to cross, to ensure I've followed my suggestions. Sometimes I go back and write "bad idea" or "no pollen" to indicate ideas I've thrown out, or the fact that neither proposed parents have pollen. This is my most fun notebook and is good for those nights of insomnia –that's why it's next to my bed!

The selected seedlings are transplanted to an observation bed after bloom is over, leaving them as clumps for the next season. The clump effect of dwarf and median irises is an important one, so I like to observe that before separating them into single rhizomes for introduction to the public through catalogs and the internet.

Establishing a Breeding Program

After you have made a few pretty crosses and raised a few groups of seedlings, you are ready to graduate from a simple pollen dauber to a hybridizer. You may have found some interesting seedlings in your first patches of seedlings. Now you need to establish a program so that the chances for producing a superior seedling are maximized.

So, how does one start a breeding program? One of my recent projects will give you an idea of how I approach this. At the last Portland American Iris Society Convention, one of the guest plants was Jayne Ritchie's aptly named SDB 'Guacamole', a green flower with a distinctive coloring reminiscent of the famous dip. Greens have always fascinated me; one of my first crosses as a kid was 'Green Spot' × 'Blueberry Muffins', which netted a good green with a blue beard. Green color in bearded irises is a difficult mix. Just a bit of anthocyanin overlying a lemon carotenoid base is the usual recipe for green color in irises. This is a delicate balance, and often the so-called greens are more tan or brown in some climates. When one normally thinks of green, we think chlorophyll, but that is largely confined to the leaves. The backs of the falls and sometimes the flower veins are greenish, but rarely does this cause any significant flower coloration.

In SDBs and MDBs, however, the yellow flavone pigments prominent in the spot can mix with the blue-purple anthocyanin in the vacuole of the cell to give a green color. The classic SDB 'Green Spot' is an example of this, and Bennett Jones developed a good series of green amoenas that fell out of his orange SDB lines. 'Guacamole' impressed me as the best approach to a green self (rather than a spot) in the SDBs, and the urge to fiddle with it was sparked. When I looked at the pedigree, I saw lots of plicatas, which made me a bit nervous because sometimes these odd blends are just the right mix of colors, and crosses shift the balance in unproductive and ugly ways. One of my hybridizing friends said, "I wouldn't touch it," and that was probably good advice, but at that point I was committed. Besides its unique green color, it also had unique aqua beards that I thought might be interesting to exploit. For other parents, I ordered a selection of greenish SDBs from a number of breeders. Some of these were rejected when they bloomed—they had poor growth, irregular form, or not enough buds. I decided that they weren't good subjects.

I chose 'Blue Oasis' for a parent because of its excellent form, three-four buds, and great vigor. The green color was more restricted in this flower but still obvious. 'Blue Eyed Girl' was chosen because it had a variety of yellow colors, decent form, and a strong blue beard. The first patch of seedlings came from the crosses 'Blue Oasis' × 'Guacamole' and 'Blue Eyed Girl' × 'Guacamole'. Although I would have liked bigger seedling numbers, I bloomed about fifty from the 'Blue Oasis' group and about twenty from the 'Blue Eyed Blonde' group.

In the 'Blue Oasis' group, the colors ranged from nearly white to deep violet, but there was an excellent blue-infused green with a blue beard and excellent form, and a pastel green with the aqua beard of 'Guacamole'. Although the green didn't have the form I wanted, the color was exactly what I was seeking—it was cleaner than 'Guacamole' and had some chlorophyll veining that enhanced the greenness. These two seedlings were crossed back to 'Guacamole' and sib-crossed. The seedlings

Vaughn seedling AA36-1 from 'Blue Oasis' × 'Guacamole'

Vaughn seedling AA36-2 from 'Blue Oasis' × 'Guacamole'

from the 'Blue Eyed Girl' cross were less exciting, although two seedlings with good form and a brownish-green color were saved and crossed back to 'Guacamole' too (I have less faith that this group will produce the results I want). Work on this line did not stop in 2019, while the seedlings from 2018 were growing. I made the cross to 'Blue Oasis' a dozen more times. More than two hundred seedlings resulted from the cross to 'Guacamole'. With these kinds of numbers you can monitor the full potential of the cross, maybe even including a seedling with the form of the blue-and-green combo with the color of the best green. In addition, a number of crosses of 'Guacamole' to 'Cheerful Chipmunk' and 'Psychedelic Dream' were made, which offered other approaches to greenish tones. All in all, about 450 seedlings from this SDB green project bloomed in 2021, and all sorts of green blends were obtained. A further group of seedlings should bloom in 2022 and 2023.

Although this project has just started, I am pleased with the progress and the potential for some nice things to appear.

So, to summarize the steps:

- Choose a project that interests you.
- Collect a series of plants that will aid you toward that goal.
- Assess the plants collected for quality and intercross all the good ones.
- Cross the best of the resulting seedlings back to the parents and to each other.
- Repeat these steps in successive generations, adding other useful parents along the way to augment the program.

I advocate for line breeding or inbreeding to achieve my goals. This is a longer process, but sometimes you can short-circuit this by studying pedigrees. For example, Terry Aitken's SDB 'Easy Does It' appears in a lot of MDB pedigrees, and the Hager MDB 'Self Evident', a selection from his lines of tetraploid MTBs × *pumila*, appears in that pedigree. Thus, there are lots of genes for dwarfing effects plus some new blood from the SDBs for improved form. Terry Aitken's MDB 'Tiny Beacon', a strong-purple amoena with a tangerine beard, is a descendant of 'Easy Does It', as is Thomas Johnson's clear-blue amoena 'Alas'. As soon as they bloomed, I crossed the two cultivars both ways and raised about seventy seedlings from the cross. Most of the seedlings were MDBs, and most had some sort of spot pattern on the falls, ranging from a pale blue to a near black. I repeated that cross for the next two years to see more progeny. Many were improvements on their

TOP 'Kung Fu Panda'

BOTTOM 'Little Jackpot'

parents, and the first two selections were registered as 'Kung Fu Panda' and 'Little Jackpot'. These two were intercrossed, crossed to numbered siblings, and crossed back to 'Alas' and 'Tiny Beacon'. In the spring of 2021, I had several hundred seedlings from these crosses, with many nice flowers. So, by taking advantage of the crosses of others, I was able to initiate a line of inbred MDBs and save time by not reinventing the wheel.

Although line breeding is in my wheelhouse of techniques, and one I use almost reflexively, I keep my collection current in terms of colors and patterns. Some of these new cultivars may be added to the breeding program, but I will continue the line without adding these cultivars until the line becomes stale or starts to show reduced vigor. These other cultivars also serve as benchmarks for my hybridizing.

This may sound like "never do an outcross." However, I do them all the time. When I first arrived in Oregon, I hadn't crossed diploid MTBs for some years. Armed with a good collection of new ones and some standards of the class, I began making all sorts of combinations. Some of my current lines descended from that first year of outcrossing, although other crosses gave me a fair amount of garbage. Outcrossing has the advantage of bringing in whole new combinations of genes, and often this allows for novel characteristics in the offspring. Moreover, there is often a hybrid vigor in seedlings from outcrosses, whereas in line breeding there is always the chance for loss of vigor unless you scrupulously weed out the weaklings. While the outcrossing brings together new sets of genes, line breeding is a method for refining the results of that initial outcross and examining all of its potential.

It's a Numbers Game—Beating the Odds

Plant hybridizing is a numbers game. The more progeny you raise, the more likely you are to find a worthy seedling. Most of us don't have the space that the Schreiners have to raise 20,000–40,000 seedlings, so anything you can do to increase your chances of superior progeny is a good strategy. There are several approaches to consider to maximize your chances. Several formative visits to established hybridizers during my youth influenced my thinking, and I still use those strategies.

My first trip to the Watkins garden in New Hampshire was eye-opening. Here on a hillside were beds after beds of blue and white TB irises. That alone was impressive, but what struck me was the high average quality of each seedling and the large numbers raised from a single cross. Ed and Art Watkins spent considerable time planning their crosses over the winter, and if a cross was a good idea, they not only did the cross in quantity but kept repeating it over several years to exhaust the possibilities. Because of these large numbers, recessive traits occurred, such as recessive whites that would have been impossible to obtain if only a few seedlings were raised. Although the Watkins irises were from line breeding, which sometimes signals problems with plant health, vigor was maintained through judicious selection of only the healthiest plants. Only occasionally was an iris outside their lines used in crossing, and these were often related to the irises that started the Watkins line. Working this line, they were ensured of having lots of lovely progeny every year. I don't have Watkins acreage, but I do follow their rules of making the cross multiple times and repeating it in subsequent years to exhaust the possibilities. I also keep a notebook by my bedside for recording "crossing ideas" during the bloom season. As I run to make crosses in the all-too-short bloom season, I consult this book to make sure I am making the suggested crosses. Of course, occasionally what seemed like a good idea in the winter often turns out to be a terrible one when you see the proposed parents again. One or both of the proposed parents might have a defect that you don't want to perpetuate in your seedlings. Don't be afraid to abort a bad idea! I've even ripped off set pods when I realized what horrors I might create.

A visit to Lynn Markham's garden was also pivotal. In contrast to the Watkins, her garden was cut out of a rocky hillside (actually a ledge!), and spaces to grow seedlings were limited, but the high average quality of her seedlings was impressive. Even working in small numbers she produced plants that could be named. What set Lynn apart from other small hybridizers is that she was a keen observer of the total iris package. So, she was able to identify "good form" and used few but powerful parents in her crosses, sometimes doing a "saturation program" in which a single stellar parent would be used in all combinations with a wide range of parents. Her 'Angel Feathers' served as the basis of a long and successful BB breeding program and was used as a breeding stud. When I started my BB program, I took the same approach, crossing 'Marmalade Skies' and 'Hillbilly Heaven' to every other BB and to each other. I've also learned to avoid parents with faults that might persist in later generations.

Bee Warburton's garden was magic. She had all sorts of crosses going on in a diverse set of dwarf and median irises. Although she practiced line breeding in her SDB projects, she made lots of progress in incorporating species into the gene pool. These species include *I. pumila*, *I. taurica*, *I. aphylla*, *I. attica*, and *I. aphylla*, among many others. Introductions from these lines are everywhere in the dwarf and median gene pool. We have Bee to thank for bringing *I. astrachanica* into the MTB gene pool. Her 'Tyke' showed the potential of this parent, and virtually every MTB hybridizer harnessed it. *I. astrachanica* proved to be the ultimate "headshrinker," converting too-tall and too-large-flowered diploid TBs into proper MTBs in the first generation. It has served me well in shrinking some of the unique diploids in Phil Edinger's historic TB collection into MTB size.

Bee also taught me about having "a vision." She had ideas as to the sorts of forms and colors that she wanted, and went after them. When the first luminata SDB appeared in her patch, they were quite horrible, with wretched narrow petals and poor substance. However, they had a different effect on the petal color. She described it aptly as "like having milk poured in the basic color." A less experienced breeder might have given up on them because of these faults, but Bee persisted for many generations and produced a wonderful series of luminatas. Although she never obtained the exact shade of those first ones, her 'Rosie Lulu' was close and was in a form that pleased her.

To recap these lessons learned:

- Repeat successful crosses to increase numbers, and keep repeating if good results are obtained.
- Study pedigrees and plan crosses for the next season.
- Use a proven strong parent to do a saturation program.
- Utilize species, species hybrids, or older hybrids that offer qualities you'd like to see in your seedlings.
- Have a vision. If your seedlings show you something interesting, follow that pathway to its completion.

Understanding Flower Color Genetics

Diploid MTBs

Most diploid MTBs are derived from long-ago crosses between the blue *I. pallida* and the variegata *I. variegata* (Randolph 1965). Paul Cook developed a genetic shorthand to describe these two parents on the basis of their dominant and recessive characteristics (Cook 1965; Witt 1965; Randolph 1965). The blue *I. pallida* contributes blue color to the entire flower (a self) and yellow carotenoids restricted to the beards, whereas *I. variegata* contributes yellow color to the entire flower and a dark spot of anthocyanin on the falls. Paul used the genetic shorthand of B = blue, Y = yellow, and V = variegata spot to describe these dominants. So a BYV genotype would be a sort of bicolor blend. The old name for this coloring was "squalens," taken from the name of a natural hybrid of these two species. Here are all the combinations:

BYV = bicolor blend, generally tan with deeper fall colors
BY = blend, usually a tan to brown self but can be reddish
BV = neglecta, light-blue standards and darker-blue falls
YV = variegata
V = amoena
Y = yellow
B = blue
byv = white

Let's say I'm crossing a good brown but want to improve its shape with many of the well-formed yellow MTBs. According to Paul's model, I'm ensured of getting at least half the seedlings to have brown flowers and, with any luck, the form of the yellow parent.

This is a simple model, and we know now that there are several kinds of recessive whites in the diploids, as well as several yellows. Still, it is a useful way to look at crosses. When I'm looking for parents for potential crosses, Paul's model is what's in my head as I cross MTBs.

Paul did not consider the plicata recessives in his scheme, but the plicatas can occur in any of the combinations of colors except pure white or yellow. For example, rich-brown bicolor plicatas on a yellow ground would result from coupling the plicata with BY(V) dominants. Although there are many plicata patterns found even in the diploids, we know relatively little of the genetics of plicata types. However, a cross of 'Just a Dusting', an all-over-dotted type crossed with a seedling with stitching only on the petal margins, gave a progeny with the dotting and stitching confined to the borders. Whereas most blue plicatas have a rather typical stitched-edge pattern, combining the variegata types with plicata gives interesting bicolor and bitone plicatas with sanding and dotting. The diversity of plicata patterns, even in diploids, is enormous, and it is likely that other modifying loci contribute to the location, extent, and type of pattern.

In addition to the standard blue color of *I. pallida*, their orchid-pink variants are found in the wild. They lack a colorless flavone that complexes with the anthocyanins to give a bluer color (Witt 1965 and personal communication), and the trait is inherited as a recessive to blue. Before the advent of the tangerine-pink types, these were the pinkest bearded irises. The orchid-pink color is able to exist in all backgrounds, so there are selfs ('Think Spring'), amoenas ('Razzleberry Dressing'), and plicatas ('Crafted') in orchid pink. It's harder to discern the orchid pink in some of the blends, but it's likely that some of the more pastel or pinkish ones such as 'Tyrone' and 'Breakfast in Bed' have the orchid-pink gene.

Fred Megson (Megson and Megson 1970) performed detailed studies of diploid bearded-iris genetics and found that there are at least three kinds of recessive white types. W^1, the most common, is represented by the classic MTBs 'Pewee' and 'Daystar', w^2 is found in the old classic 'La Neige', and *pl-a* in the white *I. pallida* 'Kupari'. Crosses between these types give the complementary solid-blue violets. That is, a cross of 'Daystar' (w^1 w^1 W^2 W^2) × 'La Neige' (W^1 W^1 w^2 w^2) gives blues (W^1 w^1 W^2 w^2) that have a wild-type allele at both loci.

The w^1 locus contains several alternatives to the white recessive: the maculosa pattern ('Gesundheit') of purple speckles on a light ground, and the recessive amoena pattern (w^1-*am*). Thus, crossing the many w^1 whites with these two patterns gives more of these patterns. Fortunately, we have many lovely w^1 whites in the MTBs, and they can be used to create new maculosas or amoenas by crossing these patterned flowers to w^1 whites. In some of these crosses, the w^1 dilutes the coloring of the other parent. For example, Jean Witt's cross of 'Pewee' × the strong amoena 'Mrs. Andrist' gave the pastel amoena 'Ice Fairy'. The dominance order of the alleles is w^1> w^1-*am*> w^1-*mac*> w^1.

We know less about the yellow diploids, other than that there are several types, on the basis of chromatography of the carotenoid pigments. Some are definitely more orange than others, and the

beard of 'Daystar' has been shown to contain lycopene, the pigment of pink tetraploids, although the color seems to be restricted to the beards in the diploids. The 'Daystar' phenotype is a common one among MTB seedlings, because plants of this coloration occur in many MTB crosses for me. Many of the yellows have what is referred to as the "flavescens" pattern of yellow standards and white falls edged yellow. Bee Warburton thought this may be a diploid expression of tangerine because it often occurred when she crossed diploid species onto tetraploid pinks. Megson and Megson (1975) identified three loci that control carotenoid production in diploid irises. Due to the multiple steps of carotenoid biosynthesis, it is likely there are many more genes involved.

Tetraploid BBs, MTBs, and IBs

In addition to the genes described for the diploids, several important genes are responsible for colors in the tetraploids that are not found in the diploid gene pool. You should also familiarize yourself with the differences between diploids and tetraploids in segregation. The chapter by Ken Kidd in *World of Irises* (1978) is a sound discussion of this topic.

'Maniac' is an MTB seedling of Lynda Miller's with a beautiful maculosa pattern.

The tangerine (*t*) locus is involved with conversion or diversion of carotenoid production into lycopene production, the pigment that gives color to tomatoes (Sturtevant 1951a). The original tangerine pinks were uncovered by a careful line-breeding program by Illinois hybridizer David Hall. Although originally found only in tall bearded irises, these tangerine pinks are found throughout the tetraploid and amphidiploid median and dwarf irises as well. The tangerine locus confers a number of different shades, from a true pink to a deep orange, depending on the concentration of lycopene and the presence of other carotenoids. When the tangerines are combined with anthocyanin colors, mulberries, orchids, and even browns and reddish tones are possible.

Three dominant inhibitors of anthocyanin occur in tetraploids, but not in most diploids. The *I* gene inhibits anthocyanin from the entire flower. This is the predominant type of white found in the tetraploids now (Sturtevant 1951b). Instead of producing anthocyanin, these *I* whites accumulate a colorless anthocyanin pseudobase. Treatment of petal extracts with dilute acid will convert the pseudobase to a blue anthocyanin and is a good check for the presence of this gene. Crosses of blues to *I* whites give mostly whites. Yellow and pinks are also most often *I* whites + carotenoids, because *I* eliminates any dulling or dirty overtones, especially in the yellows. It is believed that the *I* gene was brought into the TBs from *I. lutescens* by the crossing of white IBs into TB stock (Sturtevant 1951b).

The *I-s* gene was brought into the tetraploid gene pool by Paul Cook, who in crossing the dwarf species *I. reichenbachii* with tall blue iris found that the resultant hybrids had dirty white standards and blue falls. He named one of these hybrids 'Progenitor', because it was the cultivar that allowed for the production of amoenas with smooth hafts, unlike the more veined sort derived from *I. variegata* that are the prominent types in the diploids. Only a hybridizer with vision could see 'Progenitor' as a break in hybridizing, because it was a muddy, awful little iris! We refer to this as dominant amoenas to distinguish them from the recessive amoenas we see frequently in diploids. Now, virtually all the amoenas and bicolors in the tetraploids are the result of this *I-s* gene. An extreme case of these dominant amoenas is the so-called Emma Cook pattern, in which almost all flower color is eliminated from the flower, leaving only a rim of anthocyanin on the falls. The Knowlton Medal 'Christiana Baker' is a classic example. Genetic studies indicate this color pattern may be due to multiple doses of the *I-s* gene, because this pattern is found only in crosses where dominant amoenas are on both sides of the pedigree. Crosses of dominant amoenas to reds, browns, and blends result in bicolors where the standards lack anthocyanin but keep the carotenoids. So a cross of a red × a dominant amoena gives variegatas with yellow standards and red-purple falls.

The last of these inhibitors is the weakest. Paul Cook also brought this one into the tetraploid gene pool, this time from *I. imbricata*. In contrast to the *I-s* gene, the inhibitor gene from imbricata results in an intensification of color in the standards and much less color in the falls. The effect is weak, though, and strongly contrasted reverse amoenas are still rare. Bee Warburton used a *pumila* seedling with an intensification of color at the base of the standards to produce a series of reverse amoenas, including the highly contrasted 'Sky and Snow'. Reverse amoenas had occurred in some TB irises before the advent of Cook's 'Wide World', and it was one of these, the McKee blue reverse amoena TB 'Blue Angel Wings', that Bee used as a second source of reverse amoenas in her SDB lines. Combining the reverse amoena pattern with yellow or tangerine background colors creates some lovely and unusual irises with dark standards and lighter falls, such as the BB 'Cut Above'.

An IB seedling of the author's with the "Emma Cook pattern"

One allele of the plicata pattern has so far been shown to occur only in tetraploid cultivars—the luminata pattern. In essence, luminatas are the reverse image of plicatas, with anthocyanin marks between the veins, leaving the hafts, petal edges, and most of the style arm anthocyanin free. Some varieties exhibit a minimal pattern, just a few flecks on the falls, whereas others are so heavily marked they appear as dark-purple self colors from a distance. 'My Cher', the 2019 Cook-Douglas Medalist, is an outstanding example of a typical luminata pattern. Crossing luminatas to plicatas gives lumi-plics, the additive effect of both patterns, with luminata patterns between the veins and dotting and stitching at the petal edges and in the standards. Glaciatas (so-called plicata all-whites, or *pl-a*) are clear colors that lack any anthocyanin. Besides the white, they can exist with yellow or tangerine base colors, and one group of yellows called lemon-ices contains a predominance of the carotenoid xanthophyll. Because these glaciatas are the bottom recessive at the plicata locus, they can be crossed to luminatas or plicatas to give more of those patterns. One glaciata, the white mutant of *I. pallida* discovered in the former Yugoslavia by Randolph and now known as 'Kupari', is the only registered glaciata diploid, to my knowledge.

Run, Spot, Run! (with Apologies to Dick, Jane, and Sally)

One of the joys of the dwarf iris world is the patterning of anthocyanin fall spots on a wide variety of base colors. The spot has several different manifestations. The most common type is a bold spot that fills most of the falls, leaving a clean edge the same color of the base; others are more confined to an area just below the beard. The spot may also be split into a series of lines on a lighter color between the veins, or with only lines.

The original SDB and MDB plicatas descended from the unusual *pumila* 'Cretica', and the patterns found in these first plicatas were much as the TBs. Recent SDB plicatas have a more mixed source of *pumila* genes. The spot gene causes the plicata patterns to add extra markings or intensification at the site of the spot, in addition to more-typical plicata markings in the remainder of the flower.

Many workers have tried to move the spot pattern up into the taller median classes. Robert Schreiner was one of the first to attempt this. His IBs 'Drummer Boy' and 'Cutie' have bold spots of deep blue on a blue and white ground color, respectively. The next-generation cross to the TBs or BBs is where the spot pattern generally seems to be lost, because it is located on one of the four chromosomes that are nonhomologous with the TBs. The most successful approaches involved the Blyth IB 'Zing Me', which has a strong spot pattern and, for an IB, fairly high fertility. Baumunk's 'Zingerado' and Blyth's 'Lyrique' have some of the strongest spots but suffer a bit formwise: 'Zing Me' has wide-open standards that pass to its progeny. Despite these problems, the BBs descended from 'Zing Me' are showy and much in-class. It would be worth the effort to improve the form of these lines while retaining the bold spots.

Multiple Genes

Although many traits are inherited simply, a majority are controlled by multiple genes. Traits such as branching, flower form, substance, size, fragrance, and bloom season are controlled by multiple genes. A number of less important modifier genes are also involved. These create a full range of phenotypes for each of these characters.

In a classic study of the genes involved for good iris standards, Lynn Markham (1969) identified several major genes that are responsible for "good tops," including the length of the midrib and the size and width of the standards. Fortunate combinations of these characters make classic domed standards, whereas less fortunate ones can result in standards that fall open or are too stiffly upright and narrow, creating huge gaps. In TBs, open standards are considered a fault; not so for dwarfs and smaller medians. Rather, because the flowers are observed from above, the open standards allow views of the often-beautiful style arms. Weak standards that fall over, however, are a fault in all classes.

When *I. pumila* is crossed to TBs, the resultant SDBs are much smaller than what would be the average height of a cross between 4-inch and 36-inch irises. Even in the next-generation backcross to TBs, the IBs are much smaller than the TBs. The genes for small size appear be located on *pumila* chromosomes that are homologous to the TB chromosomes. In the third backcross of IB × TB, the segregations for height, size of flower, and season of bloom show interesting segregations. So, 12-inch dwarfs with TB-sized flowers and 36-inch TBs with tiny flowers, as well as every other possible combination, are obtained in a single progeny. Many of these are not good irises, but they retain genes for smallness that are often quite respectable. Some even show the hybrid vigor of the IBs.

Many hybridizers ignore fragrance, but, luckily, many dwarfs and medians have wonderful fragrance. As a kid I had a seedling with the most amazing cinnamon fragrance that you could smell 10 feet away. Unfortunately, it was also the worst-looking flower one could imagine! I made crosses with it but decided later not to plant the pods, figuring that the seedling's other traits would cause problems for generations. Many of the dwarfs and medians have what Bee Warburton described as a "grape Kool-Aid" odor, and it was one she did not enjoy! To me, it smells like iris and is pleasant.

Novelty Irises

One of the changes that has occurred in my lifetime is the increased acceptance and much-improved form of "novelty irises." As a youth, I remember the disdain they elicited. However, hybridizers such as Ben Hager capitalized on their popularity; the splashed MTBs 'Kaleidescope' and 'Joseph's Coat Katkamier' sold better than others almost every year. People wanted "something different," as Bonnie Nichols aptly put it.

Lloyd Austin first popularized horned varieties after finding a seedling with a slight beard protrusion in Sidney Mitchell's garden. In some crosses, these horns behave as dominants, but parents with a slight detachment of the terminal beard hairs seem to be better parents for maintaining these types. My BB 'Preppy' has horned grandparents but has never shown horns, so I was more than a little surprised when a seedling from ('Orinoco Flow' × 'Preppy') × sib gave one horned progeny, indicating that the traits are recessive but were lurking in 'Preppy' and required the "detached beard" background to allow expression. Lynda Miller, Hooker and Bonnie Nichols, and Paul Black have produced horned medians recently. With all the marvelous combinations of beards, petal colors, and patterns present in the dwarfs and medians, there could be some amazing horned, spooned, and flounced dwarfs and medians in the future.

TOP A BB seedling of the author's with the beard turned into a horn

BOTTOM A seedling of Lynda Miller's with a prominent flounce

Another popular class of novelty irises is the so-called broken colors, in which spots and splashes of anthocyanin occur over a paler background. In other plants, these patterns are controlled by transposable elements, first described by Barbara McClintock in maize. These transposable elements are small pieces of DNA that intercalate themselves into genes, causing the gene to become inactive. These elements either autonomously or, by the direction of a regulatory partner gene, excise from the gene, restoring it to activity. In the diploid MTBs, I find these affecting both the *w1* and *pl* loci. Broken color from the *w1* types appear as streaks and dots in a white or yellow flower. When the transposable element jumps early, there is a broad stripe of anthocyanin on that colorless background, whereas when the transposable element moves later in development, the anthocyanin spots and stripes are small, sometimes just dots. In the plicata broken-color types, the pattern shows the same sort of pattern as in the *w1* types, but instead of a white or yellow background, the splashes and dots are on a plicata background.

In the tetraploids, the situation appears to be more complex. Most of the broken-color types seem to carry at least some plicata genes, although they are not full plicatas themselves. It may be that the plicata genes serve as the regulatory factor for these transposable elements. Regardless of the reason for this, crosses of plicatas into broken-color lines seem to produce many broken-color types. Because of the high quality of plicata medians, crosses of plicatas to broken types can improve the quality of broken-color irises.

Although what I have described are changes of anthocyanin affected by transposable elements, they may also intercalate into other genes, including the carotenoids. The MTB 'Joseph's Coat Katkamier' and BB 'Corsage' were older examples of this, and Keith Keppel's IB 'Broken Promise' is a modern example. I have seen similar carotenoid splashes in some of my diploid MTB lines, although none in a form I like.

TOP: A broken-color type with early transpositions and large streaks of anthocyanin

BOTTOM: A broken-color type with late transpositions resulting in small dots

Jean Witt forecasted that these transposable elements would serve as a promising source of new colors and patterns in iris. Transposable elements can intercalate into any gene and generate new recessive patterns at that locus. The mind boggles as to what hybridizers of the future will be able to produce.

The Anomalous Genetics of Amphidiploids

SDBs are classed genetically as amphidiploids or allotetraploids because, although they have four sets of chromosomes like a tetraploid, there are two sets of two rather than four homologous sets like in the BB, tet MTBs, and pure *pumila*. Rather, the SDBs have two sets of TB chromosomes and two sets from *pumila*. These sets of chromosomes pair with themselves, not each other. Because of this, there is no segregation for all of the chromosomes, and hence the genes associated with these chromosomes.

An example might explain this more completely. In the SDB plicatas, the two sets derived from *pumila* have the glaciata (*pl-a)* gene as two copies that were originally derived from the tiny cultivar 'Cretica.' On the other set of chromosomes, the TB parent can have any combination of two of the plicata alleles (*pl, pl-lu, pl-a*). Here are the possibilities:

From TB set of chromosomes	From *pumila* set of chromosomes	Phenotype
pl pl	*pl-a pl-a*	plicata
pl pl-a	*pl-a pl-a*	plicata
pl-lu pl-lu	*pl-a pl-a*	luminata
pl-lu pl-a	*pl-a pl-a*	luminata
pl pl-u	*pl-a pl-a*	luminata-plicata
pl-a pl-a	*pl-a pl-a*	glaciata

In tetraploid plants, all four sets may contain any plicata allele, whereas in the amphidiploid

SDBs, the genetic choices are more limited to the ones above. This loss of potential genotypes doesn't seem to have affected the diversity in SDB plicata. Indeed, they have all the patterns found in the TBs, and some unique ones. Some of the rarest SDB plicatas are those that have *pumila*-influenced spot patterns superimposed on the basic plicata pattern.

Problems and Opportunities in Each Class

MDBs

After attaining a high level of breeding activity in the 1950s through 1970s, the breeding of MDBs has fallen off substantially. Most of the MDBs of that earlier era were crosses of SDBs with *I. pumila*. The resulting hybrids were delicate and definitely in-class, with the advantage of having some TB traits passed down to them. The problem is that they had unbalanced sets of chromosomes (12-8-8-8; one TB set and three *pumila* sets). Although a few had some fertility, others were close to sterile so that breeding lines could never be established. It still might be profitable to cross some of the outstanding specimens of these classic MDBs with forty-chromosome MDBs and smaller SDBs to see if the refined size could be harnessed with modern forms and colors.

Today most of the MDBs on the market are small segregates from SDB × SDB crosses and tend to bloom later than the dwarfs from the golden age. Ben Hager introduced a second approach to overcoming the infertility of the classic MDBs. By crossing tetraploid MTBs with *pumila*, he created hybrids with forty chromosomes that contained genes from both *aphylla* and *pumila*, as well as small BBs that had dwarfing factors. These have been crucial in establishing a base of fertile hybrids that can be crossed with MDBs derived from SDBs to produce progeny that stay reliably small. Indeed, in crosses between the Hager line and MDBs derived from small SDBs, the progeny are almost all MDBs (Vaughn 2019).

Tetraploid MTBs have advanced in color and form since Ben made these original crosses, and it may be advantageous to make a few new MTB × *pumila* crosses to add a bit more genetic variability to the base.

Thanks to the number of MDBs that have fallen out of SDB breeding, we are fortunate to have virtually a full color range of MDBs. Additional improvements in form, and perhaps a gentle ruffling to the petals, would be nice next steps.

SDBs

The SDBs are certainly one of the most advanced classes of irises; they are second to TBs only in number of registrations each year. This is remarkable for a class of irises that didn't exist until the 1950s. However, these irises have inherent problems that have yet to be solved.

In many cases, SDBs have foliage that is too large or coarse, and the bloom stalks do not rise sufficiently above the foliage. Paul Black's new 'Weird Science' is a cross of *I. juonia* and offers a plant with smaller foliage and stalks well out of the foliage. SDBs often have only two or three buds, especially in some lines that go back to *I. lutescens*, such as the whites with blue spots.

A brown plicata MDB seedling of the author's

TOP A branched SDB seedling of Paul Black's, showing the potential for branching in this class

BOTTOM A repeat blooming SDB seedling of the author's from 'Fairy Fireworks' × 'My Cher'

However, there are SDBs with six or seven buds now, and these should serve as useful breeding material to incorporate into lower-budded lines. Some of the recent Paul Black seedlings have stalks that rival IBs and MTBs.

Reblooming SDBs are some of the most reliable of all the reblooming irises, but their form has not kept pace with the best one-time bloomers. Crosses of the best once-bloomers to the most consistent rebloomers are the obvious approach to producing more high-quality rebloomers. Terry Aitken's 'Fairy Fireworks' offers another approach to extending the bloom season through repeat blooming, so that it blooms with SDBs, IBs, and TBs. Seedlings from crosses of 'Fairy Fireworks' to the once-bloomer 'My Cher' were mainly repeat bloomers, indicating that this trait is heritable.

Pinks in SDBs have traditionally been a breeding problem, probably because the originals from Roberts and Brown lines had poor form and tended more toward apricot. Recent cultivars have solved these problems. Crosses of SDBs to small IBs have proven useful in producing SDBs with better form and closer to true pink. Pinks are one of the few areas in SDB breeding where some further TB or BB × *pumila* crosses might still be worth exploring. Although Bee Warburton produced laced SDBs in the 1960s and 1970s, few SDBs carry these traits, although some modern SDBs have laciniated petals, not quite lace but a similar effect. True reverse amoenas also seem to be rare in recent SDB history.

Both Bee Warburton and Paul Cook tried to produce "late dwarfs" by crossing IBs into TBs. They mostly obtained out-of-proportion plants, although Paul did find a few with acceptable size. The goal of these crosses was to produce a strain that could be used as low borders to TB beds. Recently, Paul Black has been crossing for late dwarfs and has made a lot of progress.

The SDB class is a special treat for beginners, because they are highly fertile and the seedlings have a high average quality. Even what would be considered a wide (and potentially ugly) cross in

the TBs gives pleasing results in the SDBs. Some of the color and pattern combinations are truly amazing. I have the rare good luck to live just a few miles from the seedling patches of Thomas Johnson and Paul Black, and it is such fun to see their progress.

IBs

Most of our IBs are still derived from crosses of TBs × SDBs. Such crosses are either an introduction or compost material, because so many of the IBs have limited fertility. However, not all is lost.

Marky Smith and others (Smith 1999, 2005; Loktev 2000) have done considerable IB × SDB and IB × TB or BB crosses. These yield several kinds of offspring, so classification is sometimes an issue. Gamete formation is an issue in these plants; they have an unbalanced composition of 12-12-12-8, so gametes with odd numbers of chromosomes are produced from the odd pairing of the remaining set from *pumila* and one of the sets from the TBs. It is important to use the IB as the pod parent in most cases, because IB pollen looks fluffy and normal but rarely sets pods. The pods that do set may be a contaminated cross.

ABOVE Some of the amazing seedlings of Paul Black's being readied for introduction

Loktev (2000) made a similar observation on the relative infertility of IB pollen. Using an IB as a pod parent ensures that the IB contributes to the progeny. There are numerous exceptions to the idea that IB pollen is sterile, however, going back to crosses made by Adelaide Peterson and Alta Brown in the 1960s.

The Craigs, Paul Black, and Philip Remaire have produced outstanding IBs derived from *aphylla* rather than from the traditional TB × SDB route. These have balanced sets of chromosomes and are highly fertile. They tend to be less finished flowers than traditional IBs, and a little more lax in form. What they lack in form, they make up in branching, compliments of *aphylla*. However, the latest of these IBs, such as Remaire's lovely 'Dalriada', have exquisite form and coloring and are fully fertile. These tetraploid IBs cross readily onto the classic IBs, and the progeny from those matings seems to be much more fertile than the standard IBs. As Paul Black and others have found, a dose of *aphylla* into the pedigree seems to increase the fertility of the offspring, despite what should be chromosome problems. Crosses of these fertile IBs with early-season TBs should allow all the patterns and colors of the TB to be passed on to plants of IB size and season. Best yet, lines of improvement can be established, rather than having to worry about chance working combinations between the TB and SDB parents.

TOP A luminata IB seedling of the author's

BOTTOM A minimally marked plicata seedling of the author's

MTBs

Of all the median classes, the MTBs have made the largest jump in improvement and public acceptance. For years, we suffered through a collection of drab pastels with ancient forms and plants that grew out of class and with low fertility. Today, we have a large range of cultivars with bright colors, and it is the rare diploid MTB that is not in-class in most places in the country. Moreover, most set seed with abandon, and one can begin to pursue lines.

The genetic base of the diploid MTBs is rather narrow, almost all going back to the original Williamson cultivars. Fortunately, there is a far-greater diversity within the diploid TB and BB cultivars, and even breeders early on in the development of the class these were tapped as sources for additional genes. There are still many unique diploids to be tapped. In the early days, "head-shrinkers," tiny MTBs or ones that were too short for the class, were crossed onto the diploid BBs and TBs. Jean Witt had a seedling from a bee pod on 'Pixie' that she used for this purpose. With the advent of *I. astrachanica*, though, we now have a better one. My favorite of these astrachanica derivatives is Terry Varner's 'Astra Girl'. It is the original "blank slate" as far as parents goes, since it seems to allow the colors and patterns of the other parent to shine through in the progeny. Many of my lines now involve 'Astra Girl' or an advanced-generation hybrid resulting from it. I'm also using seedlings from Stephanie Markham that incorporate the vividly marked diploid TB 'Romeo' or an unnamed diploid from Fred Mullinax dubbed "Mullinax Butterfly" in crosses. We still need more good dark colors in the MTBs, and I have seen some progress in crossing darkest purples, browns, and reds with each other. As in all classes, approaches to red are needed. Jean Witt bequeathed to me some of her reddest seedlings for this purpose. Chad Harris's two red MTBs, 'Candy Basket' and 'Black Cherry Sorbet', have fine form and color and should be useful. Jean Witt did find malvidin in several variegatas, and it is this pigment that allows for red Louisiana and Siberian irises (Vaughn and Lyerla 1978). It is hoped that more close-to-spectrum reds can be obtained through this breeding.

Dorothy Guild did much to incorporate genes from the tetraploid varieties into the diploid lines. As you might imagine, this was a difficult process because seed counts were low, and resulting seedlings often had low fertility as well. With the advent of many improved tet MTBs, crossing diploids with tetraploids became a better possibility. Thomas Johnson's red-brown 'Crossword' is from 'Sun Spirit' × 'Peebee and Jay', and 'Mystic Crystal' and 'Lavender Sprinkles' are from crosses of tets with the recalcitrant aneuploid 'Crystal Ruffles'. Although both 'Crossword' and 'Mystic Crystal' are reticent parents, 'Lavender Sparkles' seems to be fully fertile. These sorts of crosses are difficult but may be worth making in quantity so that enough fertile offspring are obtained to carry on this breeding.

The tet MTBs have also made vast improvements since the early Hager hybrids. Although many are on the tall and big-flowered end of the class, recent offerings are much more in-class. Many of these are tangerine or dominant bicolors or both. With enough small BBs and fertile IBs available, it might be wise to cross the best of these with the smallest tet MTBs. This could add new colors and patterns not yet available in the tet MTBs. Lynda Miller has already created dark flowers with red beards, plus a number of the dominant amoena and tangerine genes together in one flower.

In 2015, Jean Witt sent a letter to many of the iris hybridizers outlining areas for improvement in the diploid MTBs. The list is still relevant, although many of these improvements are appearing in patches of the MTB hybridizers. Jean recovered a couple of yellow amoenas from the diploid TBs

'Mocha Latte' is an MTB approach to brown standards and black falls.

A Lynda Miller MTB seedling in a beautiful variegata pattern

'Sylvia' and 'Pluie d'Or', but none of them exhibited MTB proportions. In most crosses between yellow MTBs, the seedlings are self-colored or yellow standards / white fall reverse bicolors; even bitone yellows are rather rare. Jean Stevens, who produced the first tetraploid TB yellow amoenas, uses crosses involving variegatas and whites to launch her project to produce this color pattern in tetraploids, even though dominant whites don't exist among the diploid MTBs. One of the original Williamson MTBs, 'Daystar', is a white flower with strong-yellow haft markings that might be pursued to increase these hafts into totally yellow falls. The old diploid 'Elsinore' has a distinct band of rose around the standards in an otherwise self lemon flower. This pattern has not been found in any MTB, although Stephanie Markham and I have boomed seedlings with bands of color around the standards; I registered one as 'Ring Around the Collar' that seems to pass this trait to its seedlings. Jean also found that the old French Dykes Medalist 'Pluie d'Or' would produce plicatas in which the markings normally associated with plicata—stitching and dotting—would appear in yellow rather than, or with, the normal anthocyanin patterns. My 'Elfin Artistry' is the beginning of this sort of marking, with tiny dots and lines in yellow as well as purple. It will be interesting to see if all-yellow plicatas may be obtained. Other colors and patterns that Jean thought should receive attention are yellows from the orange side, orchid pinks, orchid amoenas, modern versions of 'Ice Fairy', and dark navy blues. Many of us have seedlings in our patches that are steps in these directions.

BBs

The BBs arose as short selections out of the TBs. They suffered some hereditary issues, chiefly thicker stems, short branches, and out-of-proportion plants, even though some BBs selected were good fits for the class. Three approaches are currently undertaken.

Crossing the best BBs with each other appears to be a good plan. Several BBs have proven to be excellent parents for BBs: 'Miss Ruffles', 'Marmalade Skies', 'Angel Feathers', 'Miss Nellie', 'Preppy', and 'Simmer' give a majority of seedling BBs, even with TB parents. These are getting older now, and I don't know a similar list of newer BBs from strictly TB breeding that perform as well for the percentage of BBs, although Terry Aitken's 'Cut Above', 'Banana Royale', and 'Banded Gold' have proven to be solid parents.

Some of the best new BBs are coming from lines involving *I. aphylla*. What *I. aphylla* offers the BB are thinner, more-graceful stalks and a wider branching than is typical of BBs from straight TB breeding. BBs with these bloodlines tend to stay more in-class than the usual dropouts from TB crossing, especially in climates unlike those where the BB was bred. Some of the most fruitful crosses are between the reliable BBs from TB breeding with those derived from *aphylla*. In one such recent cross in my garden, all forty-seven seedlings were BBs. With that sort of consistency, lines can be selected for other flower qualities without having to worry about obtaining mostly BBs.

As mentioned earlier, the IBs from traditional TB × SDB crosses are often of reduced fertility. However, with persistence, and in particular with certain extra-fertile IBs, crosses to BBs can give a high percentage of small irises. The hybridizer has to decide whether the plants bloom early enough to be IBs or have enough of a finished flower and later bloom to be considered a BB. Prepare for some misfits, as well as some pretty flowers, if you do this type of cross.

Tetraploid IBs and MTBs are also useful to cross onto BBs and small TBs to obtain BBs. Again, seedlings are apt to span several classes, and it is up to the hybridizer to classify the plants properly. Some of the tet MTB × BB crosses are not sophisticated enough in the F1 to be classified as BBs. In general, they need another generation of crosses, although some cultivars, such as 'Stylish Choice', are fine flowers and good fits for the BB class. Philip Remaire's sibling to 'Dalriada' is an outstanding example of this.

TBs have been bred for size at the expense of buds, but there is no reason that BBs can't reverse this trend and produce lots of buds. Certainly, we are seeing a lot more BBs with excellent stalks instead of the clubby stalks with stubby branches seen in the early days of the class.

Whatever class of medians or dwarfs you hybridize, keep it fun. It is a wonderful hobby, and the allure of creating something that might show up in gardens around the world is what keeps us going.

REFERENCES

Cook, P. "Color in Diploid Breeding." *The Medianite* 6 (1965): 56.

Guenther, G. "A Note by Mrs. John Guenther." In *The World of Little Irises*. Vol. 1. Edited by W. Welch, 86. Portland, IN: Dwarf Iris Society, 1968.

Kidd, K. K. "Iris Genetics." In *The World of Irises*. Edited by B. Warburton and M. Hamblen, 375–415. Wichita, KS: American Iris Society, 1978.

Loktev, S. "Crosses with Intermediates: More on Intermediate Fertility." *Bulletin of the American Iris Society* 317 (2000): 102–103.

Markham, L. "Iris Tops." *Bulletin of the American Iris Society* 195 (1969): 82–84.

Megson, F. H., and M. Megson. "Complementary Genes for Purple." *The Medianite* 11 (1970): 18–20.

Megson, F. H., and M. Megson. "Complementary Genes for Yellow." *The Medianite* 16 (1975): 76–78.

Randolph, L. F. "Further Commentary." *The Medianite* 6 (1965): 59–60.

Smith, M. "Fertile Intermediates: A Shattered Myth." *Bulletin of the American Iris Society* 313 (1999): 65–68.

Smith, M. "Intermediate Bearded Fertility Study, 2004." *Bulletin of the American Iris Society* 337 (2005): 74–82.

Sturtevant, A. H. "Notes on the Tangerine Beard." *Bulletin of the American Iris Society* 123 (1951a): 101–102.

Sturtevant, A. H. "Three Kinds of White Bearded Iris." *Bulletin of the American Iris Society* 123 (1951b): 99–100.

Van Ness, H. "Notes on Pigments." In *The World of Little Irises*. Vol. 1. Edited by W. Welch, 110–114. Portland, IN: Dwarf Iris Society, 1968.

Vaughn, K. C. "Are the SDB-Derived MDBs True Breeding?" *Dwarf Iris Society Portfolio* 28 (2019): 12–13.

Vaughn, K. C., and T. A. Lyerla. "Flavonoid Genetics of the 28-Chromosome 'Siberian' Iris." *Theoretical & Applied Genetics* 51, no. 5 (1978): 247–248.

Witt, J. "Color in Diploids—Notes and Comment." *The Medianite* 6 (1965): 57–58.

A BB or small TB sibling to 'Dalriada'

allele. Choices of a gene for a given trait. For example, plicata, luminata, and glaciata are all allele choices at the plicata locus.

amoena. An iris with white standards and colored falls. A reverse amoena is when the standards are colored and the falls lack anthocyanin.

amphidiploid. An iris with two sets of diploid chromosomes, such as the SDBs that have two sets of TB chromosomes and two sets of *pumila* chromosomes.

aneuploid. Having an uneven number of chromosomes, either more or less than a full set. For example, the nearly sterile MTB 'Crystal Ruffles' has one extra chromosome.

anther. Pollen-bearing area of the stamen. In bearded iris there are two locules that bear pollen.

anthocyanin. A group of red to blue pigments that are water soluble and occur in the vacuole. In some dark flowers, the pigments are concentrated in a vacuolar inclusion called the anthocyanoplast.

bicolor. All combinations of colors with standards of one color and falls of a darker color. A reverse bicolor has the same color combos, but with standards deeper.

bitone. Standards and falls of the same general hue but darker in the falls. A reverse bitone has standards darker than the falls.

blend. An iris flower showing both anthocyanin and carotenoid colors overlying each other. Anthocyanins accumulate in the epidermis, whereas carotenoids are found in subepidermal cells.

carotenoid. A group of yellow to red pigments that occur in small cellular bodies called chromoplasts

dark top. An iris flower with dark-colored standards relative to the falls, such as purple standards and yellow falls

dehisce. The opening of the suture on anthers, allowing the pollen to escape

diploid. Having two sets of chromosomes. Most MTBs are diploids. Often abbreviated "dip."

dominant. Refers to a gene choice that expresses itself regardless of other alleles

Emma Cook pattern. Named after the TB that was an early example of this pattern. It has anthocyanin expressed only as a fine edge of anthocyanin around the falls.

falls. The three lower petals of the iris flower. Technically they are sepals, but this term is rarely used to describe an iris flower.

fan. The accumulation of leaves of the iris plant

flavone. A group of iris pigments from colorless to yellow. Unlike the carotenoids, they occur in the vacuole and can complex with anthocyanins to cause truer blue or green effects, depending on the flavones.

form. The basic shape of the flower, but also used to describe a selection of a species iris distinct from others

glaciata. This is the group term for so-called ice-whites, lemon-ices, and other recessives at the plicata locus. Glaciatas appear especially clear because of the absence of all anthocyanins.

haft. The constricted area on the falls where they meet the standards. This is often the site of annoying markings that detract from the flower, but they can be a pretty feature if they are contrasted or smooth.

inbreeding. Repeated self, backcrossing to parents, or siblings

inhibitor. In the genetic sense, these are genes that cause a pigment not to be produced, or to be produced in certain areas.

locus. The site on a chromosome for a given trait—for example, the plicata locus

luminata. A pattern of spots and fine lines of anthocyanin that occur between the veins, leaving the hafts, styles, and petal edges without any markings. In essence, it is the reverse of plicata. The luminata and plicata patterns can appear together to produce an effect that occurs over all areas of the flower.

lycopene. This is the carotenoid pigment that occurs in tomatoes, but also in red bearded white and pink iris flowers.

maculosa. An irregular pattern of splashes and dots of anthocyanin on a paler background

neglecta. Standards light blue, falls dark blue / purple

novelty iris. Irises with horns, spoons, flounces, broken color, and unusual forms such as flat forms. Novelty irises are not restricted to bearded irises but occur in all types.

plicata. A pattern of anthocyanin stitching or dotting, usually restricted to the petal edges but sometimes an all-over dotted pattern

rebloomer. An iris that blooms in the spring but also sends up additional blooms in the summer or fall after a rest. Compare with repeat bloomer.

recessive. Refers to a gene choice that is not observed when a dominant allele is present. Many, but not all, white irises are recessives.

repeat bloomer. An iris that continues to bloom after the initial bloom, thus extending the bloom season

rhizome. Technically an underground storage stem that in irises anchors the plant and the places where the roots are attached

self. An iris with standards and falls the same color. Also an iris crossed with its own pollen.

space-age iris. A term introduced by hybridizer Lloyd Austin to describe irises with beard appendages called horns, spoons, or flounces

stamen. The pollen-bearing structure of the flower, divided into a stalklike filament and the pollen-bearing anther

standards. The upper three petals of the iris flower

stigma. The site on the flower where pollen is accepted and pollen germination starts. In irises it takes the form of a lip of tissue on the style arm.

style. These occur as three elongated structures in the center of the flower and house the stigma, the site where pollen is accepted.

tetraploid. Four sets of chromosomes, all with the same number in each set. Often abbreviated "tet."

variegata. Standards yellow, falls red or purple

Sources

for Dwarf and Median Bearded Irises

Aitken's Salmon Creek Garden
608 NW 119th Street
Vancouver, WA 98685-3802
www.flowerfantasy.net
(own introductions plus those of Chuck Bunnell, Chad Harris, Stephanie Markham, Marky Smith, Kevin Vaughn, and Jean Witt)

Blue J Iris
40 Palomino Road
Vado, NM 88072
www.bluejiris.com
(own introductions)

Cascadia Gardens
3011 134th Avenue NE
Lake Stevens, WA 98208
www.cascadia-gardens.com
(introductions of Lee Walker and Elm Jensen)

Chuck Chapman Iris
RR #1, 8790 WR124
Guelph, Ontario, Canada N1H 6H7
www.chapmaniris.com
(own introductions)

C&T Iris Patch
20524 CR 76
Eaton, CO 80515
candtirispatch.com
(historical as well as modern)

Eagle Ridge Gardens
www.eagleridge.com
(some historical as well as modern)

Hillcrest Gardens
3365 Northaven Road
Dallas, TX 75229
www.hillcrestiris.com
(own introductions)

Horton Iris Garden
PO Box 1054
Loomis, CA 95650
www.hortonirisgarden.com
(some historicals)

Iris City Gardens
7675 Younger Creek Road
Primm Springs, TN 38476
www.iriscitygardens.com
(some historicals)

Iris Sisters Farm
3769 Cordon Road NE
Salem, OR 97305
iris-sisters.com
(own introductions plus those of Philip Remaire)

Keith Keppel Iris
PO Box 18154
Salem, OR 97305
www.keithkeppeliris.com
(own introductions plus those of Philip Remaire)

Lauer's Flowers
PO Box 183
Independence, OR 97351
www.lauersiris.com
(own introductions)

Mid-America Garden
PO Box 9008
Brooks, OR 97305-0008
www.mid-americagarden.com
(own introductions plus those of Paul Black, Barry Blyth, and Lynda Miller)

Schreiners Iris Garden
3625 Quinaby Road NE
Salem, OR 97303
www.schreinersgardens.com
(own introductions)

Stout Gardens at Dancing Tree
432 NE 70th Street
Oklahoma City, OK 73105
www.Stoutgardens.com
(own introductions plus those of Michele Bersillon, Anita Moran, and Robert Skaggs)

Superstition Iris Gardens
2536 Old Hwy. Dept. A15
Cathey's Valley, CA 95306
Check their Facebook page
(own introductions)

Sutton's Iris Gardens
PO Box 790
Star, ID 83669
www.suttoniris.com
(own introductions)

Wildwood Gardens
PO Box 250
Molalla, OR 97038
www.wildwoodgardens.net

Winterberry Gardens
1225 Reynolds Road
Cross Junction, VA 22625-1726
www.winterberryirises.com
(own introductions)

Annotated Bibliography

Here are a few of my favorite iris books that I think you will want as part of your iris library.

Austin, C. *Irises: A Gardener's Encyclopedia*. Portland, OR: Timber, 2005. The author runs a major iris nursery in the UK, and her book covers all irises.

Grosvenor, G. *Iris: Flower of the Rainbow*. Kenthurst, Australia: Kangaroo, 1997. Beautiful illustrations of irises and a fanciful look at hybridizing.

Norris, K. D. *A Guide to Bearded Irises: Cultivating the Rainbow*. Portland, OR: Timber, 2012. Kelly is an enthusiastic grower of all bearded irises. This book features photos of many of the species and historical irises as well as the author's favorites.

Price, M. *The Iris Book*. Princeton, NJ: Van Nostrand, 1966. Although this is not a long book, it is crammed with good information and is well written.

Valette, W. *Iris Culture and Hybridizing for Everyone*. Chicago: Adams, 1961. This book represents a collection of information from thousands of iris breeders and growers from around the country. Although centering on tall bearded, it has quite a good discussion of the state of dwarfs and medians in the early 1960s.

Vaughn, K. C. *Beardless Irises: A Plant for Every Garden Situation*. Atglen, PA: Schiffer, 2015. This book covers the many beardless iris species and cultivars that complement the irises described in this book. Also has an extensive section on hybridizing and raising irises from seed.

Warburton, B. A., and M. Hamblen. *The World of Irises*. Wichita, KS: American Iris Society, 1978. A comprehensive book on all irises. The chapter on genetics is especially valuable.

Index

About the Author

Kevin C. Vaughn has grown and hybridized irises for over five decades and was mentored by many of the giants in the iris world. Having gardened in Massachusetts, Mississippi, and Oregon, he has studied iris culture in diverse growing conditions. Kevin has a PhD in plant genetics and spent 30 years working for the USDA as a plant cell biologist. In Kevin's yard, nothing with pollen is safe from his hybridizing; over 200 varieties of his plants are on the market, including daylilies, hostas, spiderworts, sempervivum, and of course irises. His two other books for Schiffer include *Beardless Irises: A Plant for Every Garden Situation* and *Sempervivum: A Gardener's Perspective of the Not-So-Humble Hens-and-Chicks*.